The House of Trials

Ibérica

A. Robert Lauer
General Editor

Vol. 21

PETER LANG
New York • Washington, D.C./Baltimore
Bern • Frankfurt am Main • Berlin • Vienna • Paris

Sor Juana Inés de la Cruz

The House of Trials

A Translation of
Los empeños de una casa
by David Pasto

PETER LANG
New York • Washington, D.C./Baltimore
Bern • Frankfurt am Main • Berlin • Vienna • Paris

Library of Congress Cataloging-in-Publication Data

Juana Inés de la Cruz, Sister, 1651–1695.
[Empeños de una casa. English]
The house of trials/ David Pasto (translator).
p. cm. — (Ibérica; v. 21)
Includes bibliographical references.
I. Pasto, David. II. Title. III. Series: Ibérica (New York, N.Y.); vol. 21.
PQ7296.J6E413   862—dc20   96-25575
ISBN (hardcover) 0-8204-3102-8
ISBN (paperback) 0-8204-6164-4
ISSN 1056-5000

Die Deutsche Bibliothek-CIP-Einheitsaufnahme

Juana Inés de la Cruz, Sister, 1651–1695.
The house of trials/ Sor Juana Inés de la Cruz. David Pasto (transl.).
– New York; Washington, D.C./Baltimore; Bern;
Frankfurt am Main; Berlin; Vienna; Paris: Lang.
(Ibérica; Vol. 21)
ISBN 0-8204-3102-8
NE: GT

© 1997, 2002 Peter Lang Publishing, Inc., New York

All rights reserved.
Reprint or reproduction, even partially, in all forms such as microfilm,
xerography, microfiche, microcard, and offset strictly prohibited.

Acknowledgements

I wish to thank Dr. Lisa Pasto-Crosby for her assistance in translating obscure passages in the text.

I also appreciate the support of the Department of Speech and Theatre at Oklahoma City University, the Association for Hispanic Classical Theatre, and Dr. A. Robert Lauer.

Special thanks go to my wife and inspiration, Dr. Alicia Kae Koger, who encouraged me to begin this project and helped edit the final draft.

Table of Contents

A Brief Biography of Sor Juana	1
The Festival of *The House of Trials*	7
Asides and Self-Reflection in *The House of Trials*	13
Feminist Interpretations of *The House of Trials*	19
Bibliography	28
The House of Trials	33
Act I	36
Notes for Act I	67
Act II	71
Notes for Act II	104
Act III	107
Notes for Act III	148

A Brief Biography of Sor Juana

Sor Juana Inés de la Cruz was born in San Miguel de Nepantla, Mexico as Doña Juana Ramírez de Asbaje. Although her first biographer, Jesuit Diego Calleja, claimed she was born on November 12, 1651, baptismal records suggest that she was born three years earlier in 1648. Her parents never married and her father seems to have disappeared when she was young, so she was raised on her maternal grandfather's hacienda (a plantation worked by Native American and Black slaves). She learned to read when she was only three and spent as much time as possible reading the books in her grandfather's library. After only twenty formal lessons, she learned enough Latin to complete her study of the language on her own.

Juana wanted to study at the renowned university in Mexico City, but all institutions of higher learning admitted only men. She begged her mother to let her dress in men's clothing so that she could attend the university, but her mother refused. Since women could not receive any formal training beyond an elementary level, Juana taught herself almost everything she knew. Without a teacher to guide her, Juana read whatever interested her, so her education was surprisingly broad, and she was extremely well-read. Allusions in her work prove she knew all the major Greek, Latin, and Spanish authors (although she could only read the Greek authors in translation). She was also well-versed in Neo-Scholasticism, the major theological movement in seventeenth-century Spain and its colonies. She may have studied music and mathematics, since she owned many musical and mathematical instruments. By her own admission, she observed natural phenomena and possessed a scientific mind as well.

In addition to her intellectual achievements, Juana was charming and witty—a clever conversationalist—and beautiful as well. These attributes, along with her intellect, helped her to find a place at the elegant and cultivated viceregal court in Mexico City. In 1664, she became a lady-in-waiting to the Viceroy's wife, the Marquise de Mancera, and was favored by both the Viceroy and the Vicereine.

> Her diplomatic arts, her beauty, her vivaciousness, and her sunny nature do not entirely explain the secret of her popularity. Intelligence and learning opened the doors of the viceregal society to her. (Paz, 96)

She lived in the viceregal palace during her adolescent years from 1664 to 1667.

Jesuit Diego Calleja claimed that the Viceroy, either for amusement or to display his wife's protégée, arranged for a dramatic test of Juana's intellect. The Viceroy

> called together at the palace some forty learned men—professors at the University, theologians, philosophers, poets, writers, mathematicians and historians—for the purpose of conducting an examination of her proficiency in the subjects of their respective specialization. The result of this contest was a triumphant rout of the inquisitors by the Marquesa's little lady-in-waiting, a success which the Viceroy never tired of describing. Years later in Spain he was to say: "In the manner of a royal galleon defending itself against a few small sloops that had assailed it, did Juana Inés free herself of the questions, arguments and objections that so many, each in his own class, propounded." (Royer, 27–8)

While the story may be apocryphal (derived from the Biblical tale of the Christ child in the Temple or the famous trial of Saint Catherine of Alexandria, the saint with whom Sor Juana most clearly identified herself), it nevertheless reveals the contemporary fascination with Juana's knowledge, wit, and self-assurance. A woman of such courage and intellect would have been viewed as a freak in the highly patriarchal society of New Spain.

Despite her fame at court, Juana entered the Convent of the Discalced Carmelites of Saint Joseph in 1667. The disciplines of this order were apparently too harsh for her, and she left three months later. In 1669, she entered the Convent of Saint Jerome, a more relaxed order, where she took her vows and remained until her death. While several clerical biographers have tried to argue that Sor Juana was a mystic, she herself does not claim that she entered the convent due to any religious zeal, and later the Bishop of Puebla, in the guise of a letter from Sister Philotea, rebuked her for not showing enough interest in spiritual matters.

In the *Respuesta a Sor Filotea* (*The Reply to Sister Philotea*) dated 1691, Sor Juana stated that one of the reasons why she entered a convent was "the total antipathy I felt for marriage" (Peden, 49). She never explained this antipathy and biographers have suggested everything from unrequited love to lesbianism as justifications for her strong aversion to marriage. Scholars do not know enough about her personal life to either prove or disprove any of these claims. (Some biographers use the erotic overtones of the love poetry addressed to the Countess of Paredes as proof of Platonic friendship, and others as proof of her homosexuality.) Electa Arenal, in her article "The Convent as Catalyst for Autonomy," offers the best explanation for Sor Juana's religious vocation:

> For centuries, most of the women who in Virginia Woolf's phrase had "a room of their own" found it in the cloister. . . . The cloister, which common opinion often represents as a refuge (or as a prison), was equally a place in which women could support each other and even cultivate a certain amount of independence. It provided women of greatly divergent personalities with a semiautonomous culture in which they could find sustenance, exert influence, and develop their talents they never could have expressed as fully in the outside world. (149)

Sor Juana supports this theory in her *Reply* where she explains her desire to live alone, "to have no obligatory occupation that would inhibit the freedom of my studies, nor the sounds of a community that would intrude upon the peaceful silence of my books" (Peden, 49–51). The convent offered Sor Juana the only respectable and honorable profession that would allow time for the study she desired.

The convents in Mexico City during Sor Juana's lifetime provided women with the only possible outlet for their intellectual or literary talents. Marcus Burke, in the catalog published to accompany the art exhibit *Mexico. Splendors of Thirty Centuries*, describes the cultural life in such a convent:

> One of the most remarkable aspects of Mexican society in the late seventeenth and eighteenth centuries was the development of what can only be called a feminist culture in many urban orders of nuns. In

> contrast to the relatively uniform austerity of Spanish institutions, Mexican convents offered a wide variety of experiences to women seeking an alternative to the traditional roles of wife and mother, as well as to those with a more traditional religious calling. . . . A number of the women, such as Sor Juana Inés and Madre María Ana Agueda de San Ignacio (1695–1756), also became literary figures, maintaining personal libraries and publishing influential works. (352)

Given the choice of a traditional role of wife and mother with little possibility of time or encouragement for intellectual and literary achievement or a life of study, culture, and respect within the walls of a convent, Sor Juana chose the only viable option available to her.

Life at the Convent of Saint Jerome was hardly austere. Alan Trueblood describes the living conditions as comfortable and hospitable to intellectual pursuits:

> The nuns had private living quarters, usually occupying two floors, with their own kitchens, baths, sleeping quarters, and parlors. They brought servants with them—in Sor Juana's case a mulatto slave-girl given to her by her mother. Juana's parlor became her study, where she amassed her own library and spent hours reading, studying, reflecting, and writing. (5)

While Sor Juana did have duties related to convent life (including two terms as convent treasurer), she had at least one slave and a two-story apartment of her own. She could devote several hours each day to reading and writing. One of her more pleasant duties was to take charge of the musical and dramatic presentations celebrating religious holidays in the convent, and she wrote many lyrics for hymns to be sung on these occasions.

Although living in the Convent of Saint Jerome under a vow of enclosure that would not allow her to go outside the convent, Sor Juana remained a part of court life. The Viceroy and Vicereine, as well as other members of the court, visited the convent frequently to attend vespers, hear the musical and dramatic presentations, and chat in the locutory. Sor Juana was the center of a *salón* that regularly met to engage in social, cultural, and intellectual conversation.

Octavio Paz notes the exclusively patriarchal nature of society and culture in New Spain and the extreme difficulty any woman would have in entering that phallocentric world. He writes:

> The only means by which women might penetrate the closed world of masculine culture was to slip through the half-open doors of the court and the Church. Although it may seem strange, the two places where men and women could congregate for the purpose of intellectual and aesthetic communication were the convent locutory and the palace drawing room. Sor Juana made use of both of them. (45)

A few biographers have viewed Sor Juana's vocation as shrewd hypocrisy and her many letters in praise of the Vicereine as cunning flattery, but these men do not acknowledge the difficulties of being an independent and intelligent woman in seventeenth-century New Spain. She needed the respectability of the convent and the favor of the court in order to pursue her studies and her writing.

The Spanish King appointed Viceroys for three-year terms (occasionally re-appointing them for one or two more three-year terms), and Sor Juana was fortunate to find several viceregal households that favored her. The Marquis and Marquise of Mancera, her first patrons, ruled from 1664 to 1673. The next Viceroy, Archbishop Payo Enríque de Ribera, was friendly and protective towards Sor Juana and visited her in the convent both before and during his term as Viceroy. The Count and Countess of Paredes (also referred to as the Marquis and Marquise de la Laguna), who served from 1680 to 1686, were as enthusiastic about Sor Juana as the Marquis and Marquise de Mancera. During their term of office, Sor Juana experienced her most productive years as a writer, and the Countess of Paredes published Sor Juana's works in Spain after returning to Europe. The viceroys who followed the Count of Paredes had less interest in the arts and needed to focus their attention on the famine, plague, and riots that Mexico suffered at the time. The loss of viceregal favor, coupled with the hostility of the Archbishop of Mexico, Francisco de Aguiar y Seijas (a powerful man who hated secular drama as well as women), led to problems for Sor Juana later in life.

In her *Reply to Sister Philotea*, Sor Juana described her passion for learning and defended the right of women to pursue their studies. The *Reply* serves as an early feminist treatise written with style and wit, and abounds with evidence of her scholarship and intellect. Sor Juana included a great deal of autobiographical material in the *Reply*, which serves as a major source for facts about her life.

Scholars do not know whether or not Sor Juana continued to study in the two years following the *Reply*, although they do know she wrote a hymn in praise of Saint Catherine of Alexandria. In any case, a general confession written in blood in 1693 indicates that she renounced her studies at that time and surrendered her huge library and all her musical and mathematical instruments to the misogynous Archbishop Aguiar y Seijas to be sold for the benefit the poor. The plague that raged through Mexico City entered the convent in 1695, and Sor Juana ministered to her dying sisters. She fell ill and died of the plague on April 17, 1695.

Scholars debate the reasons why she renounced her studies and sold her library. The loss of viceregal favor, the misogyny of the Archbishop of Mexico, the tyranny of her confessor (Jesuit Antonio Núñez de Miranda), the rigors of the plague, famine, and insurrections, an increase in religious superstition at the time, a true religious conversion, and even menopause have been suggested by biographers. As Gerard Flynn notes,

> Most "sorjuanists" have written a series of impressions that tell us more about themselves than about the Mexican nun, with the result that a kaleidoscopic slew of opinions exists by which Sor Juana becomes pantheistic, Catholic, Cartesian, Scholastic, mystical, irreligious, generous, selfish, candid, and hypocritical. Sor Juana is apt to become whatever her critics will her to be. (13)

In any case, various forces prevented Sor Juana from continuing her studies and she abandoned them.

Whatever Sor Juana's reasons for renouncing her writing and her studying, she remains a remarkable woman. In an era of strict religious orthodoxy, political repression, and patriarchal culture, she managed to do what few other women of her time could do: she had a career and achieved fame as a poet and dramatist. Her contradictory nature—nun and politician, erotic poet and treasurer, scientist and playwright, proto-feminist and submissive daughter of the Church—fascinates biographers who find their lives mirrored in hers. Whatever the truth, she deserves her honorific titles as "the Tenth Muse" and "the Phoenix of America."

The Festival of *The House of Trials*

The *comedia de enredo* (comedy of intrigue) translated here as *The House of Trials* served as the centerpiece for a larger entertainment referred to as the *festejo de Los empeños de una casa*, the Festival of *The House of Trials*. The complete performance consisted of seven short works in addition to the three acts of *The House of Trials*. During the Golden Age, *comedias* were always presented in the public theatres with a prologue before the *comedia* and interludes, dances, and songs between the acts of the *comedia*. These musical numbers and interludes were rarely written by the author of the *comedia* and bore no relationship to the action or theme of the *comedia*. In contrast to typical Golden Age theatrical practice, Sor Juana wrote all of the shorter works, creating a loosely-connected, Baroque, theatrical festival.

The Festival began with a *loa* (prologue) in which four allegorical characters, Fortune, Merit, Diligence, and Chance, attempt to determine the true source of happiness. The refrain in the *loa*, "Which is the greatest happiness?", echoes the refrain of Ana's entertainment in Act II of the *comedia*, "What is the greatest pain of love?" The greatest happiness, according to the *loa*, derives from the nobility of the authorities who grant happiness—the viceroy and vicereine of Mexico, who were Sor Juana's patrons. The *loa* ends with praise for the newly-arrived Archbishop of Mexico, Don Francisco de Aguiar y Seijas.

The flattery of superiors continues in the three *letras* (poems or songs) which appear before each of the three acts of the *comedia*. The first two *letras* honor María Luisa, the Countess of Paredes and the Vicereine. The third *letra* praises the Countess' three-year-old son, José. Sor Juana owed her position at court to the Countess' goodwill and influence, and the *letras* extol the beauty, kindness, and intelligence of the Countess.

Between Acts I and II, the first *sainete* (interlude) appears with the subtitle, "At the Palace." The first *sainete* uses allegorical characters, as in the *loa*, in an unusual contest to win a woman's scorn. Catherine Larson points out, "While this *sainete* is not directly linked to the action of the main play, it nonetheless deals with the game-of-love mentality that rules in *Los empeños*" (186). Octavio Paz views the first *sainete* as a depiction of the *galanteo de palacio* (courtly flirtation) Sor Juana would have observed at court (see 91–96) but sees little connection to the plot of the *comedia*. Although unrelated to the action of *The House of Trials*, the first *sainete* may depict Sor Juana's disillusionment with life at court according to Anthony M. Pasquariello in "The Seventeenth-Century Interlude in the New World Secular Theater" (106–7).

In the second *sainete*, a group of bored audience members hiss and whistle during an interlude for a dull play (a version of the Golden Age classic, *The Celestina*) by a playwright called Acevedo. Acevedo enters and tries to defend his work, but the mob jeers him off-stage. Pasquariello notes, "There is sufficient evidence to support the conjecture that the Acevedo of the *sainete* was none other than Francisco de Acevedo [a playwright and contemporary of Sor Juana]" (107). This interlude-within-an-interlude is a clever piece of ironic self-awareness and a satire on theatre in Sor Juana's time. Catherine Larson notes, "This *sainete*, which not inconsequentially comes between Acts II and III of *Los empeños de una casa*, even pokes fun at the character [in Acevedo's play] who played the role of a woman (here, the Celestina), in an obvious foreshadowing of Castaño's role in Act III when he dresses as a woman and breaks the scenic fiction to talk directly to the audience" (186). The second *sainete*, with its satire on the theatre in general and the portrayal of women in particular, is the only piece of the Festival that directly comments on the *comedia*.

The entire Festival ends with the *sarao de cuatro naciones* (the Masque of Four Nations), a musical entertainment in which four ethnic groups sing the praises of New Spain and the Viceroy. This elaborate spectacle of song and dance has no connection to the action of *The House of Trials*, and serves only as another piece of flattery. Baroque court theatre often paid such direct and elaborate homage to its patrons.

Most critics who comment on the *loa, sainetes, letras,* and *sarao* find little to praise in them. Gerald Flynn summarizes the general opinion of the *loa* when he says, "The dramatic action between the abstract figures is forced, most of the verses are wooden, and the last hundred-odd verses are a mechanical tribute to the new rulers" (53). He dismisses the three *letras* saying, "Like the *loa* before them, they lack poetic inspiration" (54). He continues his critique with the observations that the first *sainete* is "too contrived and abstract to be considered good theatre" (54), and that the *sarao* is "dull" (55). In his article on the interludes, Pasquariello concedes that "both *sainetes* are not entirely free of the gongoristic curse which reduced colonial expression to a labyrinth of formula rhetoric and wordplay" (106). Only the second *sainete* is praised by most critics, and Octavio Paz thinks it is one of Sor Juana's best dramatic works. Although the short dramatic works in the Festival of *The House of Trials* fall prey to ornate, tortured syntax and elaborate, strained conceits in imitation of the influential Spanish poet Luis de Argote y Góngora (1561–1627), the three acts of *The House of Trials* remain relatively free of such dense and undramatic poetry, except when Sor Juana uses overly ornate langauge to characterize Don Rodrigo's speech.

The short dramatic works of flattery that appeared before, between, and after the *comedia* might have pleased a seventeenth-century audience which would have expected such entertainments, but they have little relevance for a modern audience. Catherine Larson, the only English-speaking critic who seems to appreciate any of the short pieces except the second *sainete,* concedes:

> It should be noted, however, that the decision to include these pieces with a staging of the play could pose a serious pragmatic problem for a director and producer. Contemporary audiences, unaccustomed to such protracted performances would probably balk at attending a production of the entire *festejo*.(186)

This practical consideration, plus the questionable literary and dramatic merit of most of the short pieces, lead to exclusion of these pieces from this translation. For modern readers as well as audiences, the short pieces would only interrupt the swift flow of action in the *comedia*.

The *loa, sainetes, letras,* and *sarao* that accompanied *The House of Trials* reflect the tradition of dramatic festivals for special occasions that developed in the New World. Pasquariello notes:

> Performances in the viceregal courts of both colonial capitals [Lima and Mexico City] added considerably to the general theatrical activity. The arrival of a new Viceroy, Archbishop, or eminent royal patrons, the birthdays and anniversaries of members of the royal families, and holy days were events which called for sumptuous festivities usually culminating with performances of *comedias, autos sacramentales*, interludes and *loas* in the reception hall of the palace for the pleasure of the royal gathering. (105)

These private performances in the palace or homes of the nobility served to display the wealth and taste of the viceregal court and to flatter the reigning or newly arrived political, social, and religious authorities.

The entire Festival of *The House of Trials* premiered in Mexico City on October 4, 1683, according to Alberto G. Salceda, in his introduction to the fourth volume of Sor Juana's complete works published in 1957. He bases his argument for this date on the passage in the *loa* praising the new Archbishop of Mexico, who arrived in the fall of 1683, and on a reference in the second *sainete* to Don Fernando Deza, the Collector of Taxes. Then Salceda quotes a diary entry for October 4, 1683 that mentions both the Archbishop's arrival and a festival at the house of Don Fernando Deza, and concludes:

> This allows us, then, to state, almost with complete certainty, that *The House of Trials*, with its prologue, interludes, songs, and masque, was presented in the house of the Collector, Don Fernando Deza, in Mexico, on October 4, 1683, on the occasion of a festival in honor of the Viceroy and Vicereine, the Count and Countess of Paredes, and on the date of the public entry of the new Archbishop, Don Francisco de Aguiar y Seijas. (xviii, translation by David Pasto)

The irony of Deza commissioning a woman to write a comedy to celebrate the arrival of a misogynist who opposed secular theatre is matched only by Sor Juana praising the man who, according to Octavio Paz, would silence her eight years later.

Although the play was written for a private performance in a nobleman's home, the dramatic conventions of *The House of Trials* are the same as for those for plays intended to be presented in the *corrales* (public theatres) of the Spanish Golden Age. The stage at a Madrid *corral* would have been a bare, raised platform in front of a permanent facade with several openings and a *paño* (curtain) somewhere on stage which was often used for characters to hide behind. A balcony in the facade could be used as an upper acting area and there may have been doors and windows as well. As in the Elizabethan public theatres, the Spanish Golden Age *corrales* used no illusionistic scenery. Only a few props and the descriptions in the spoken text offered any indication of the setting. No lighting effects were available on the Golden Age stage, which was lit only by sunlight. Seventeenth-century audiences would have recognized that two scenes of *The House of Trials* take place in darkness only by the performance of the actors and actresses and by the maid bringing in a light, a Golden Age convention to indicate nighttime.

Like most Golden Age playwrights, Sor Juana only vaguely indicated the settings, and critics disagree on the specifics. Paz describes the scenes in Pedro and Ana's house as all taking place in one very large, ill-defined hall or garden, Flynn calls it a garden, and Catherine Larson in her article, "Writing the Performance: Stage Directions and the Staging of Sor Juana's *Los empeños de una casa*," refers to the many rooms in the house and the continual movement of the action from one room to another. In this translation, all of the action in Pedro and Ana's house occurs in one large room with a latticed window or balcony and access to the garden and the front door. Footnotes in the text reveal where other editors have inserted scene changes. The action of the play does not require scene changes and they are not indicated by Sor Juana in the stage directions. Sor Juana, like all Golden Age playwrights, divided her play into French scenes, indicating a new scene whenever a character entered or exited. Sor Juana's French scenes serve as cues to the performers, telling them when they enter and exit, not as indications of scene changes. In terms of dramatic action, only two scenes (one in Act I between Rodrigo and Hernando and one in Act III which must take place in the street in front of Pedro and Ana's house) require a change of setting.

It is no accident that the two scenes which take place outside of the house are in the first and last acts. Sor Juana created a symmetrical structure for *The House of Trials* with Ana's musical entertainment in the middle of Act II. A scene outside of the house precedes a scene in darkness in Act I, while a scene outside of the house follows a scene in darkness in Act III. In the Festival of *The House of Trials*, Ana's musical quiz game not only served as the fulcrum of the evening's symmetry, but also provided the major link (albeit a weak one) between the *comedia* and the shorter dramatic pieces.

Sor Juana probably never saw any performance or rehearsal of the Festival of *The House of Trials* since she, like most nuns in colonial Mexico, took a vow of seclusion and never left the convent. Before becoming a nun, she might have seen the room in which the play was to be performed, but nothing in the text indicates anything special or unusual about the performance space. The text uses the same playwriting and editing conventions as appear in Lope de Vega's and Calderón's published plays.

The *comedia* and all of the shorter works in the Festival of *The House of Trials* were published in Seville in 1692 in the *Segundo volumen* [second volume] of Sor Juana's complete works. Octavio Paz believes that *The House of Trials* was also performed in Spain and throughout the Spanish empire. He documents a performance in Manila in 1709 to celebrate the birth of Philip V's first son. During nine days of bullfights, fireworks, and dances, several plays were presented, including another play by Sor Juana, *Amor es más laberinto* (*Love Is the Greater Labyrinth*), and the nine-day festival climaxed with a production of *The House of Trials* (Paz 333). No translation and consequently no production of the play ever appeared in English until this translation premiered April 20, 1995 at Oklahoma City University in a production which was directed by the translator.

Asides and Self-Reflection in
The House of Trials

In her article, "Writing the Performance: Stage Directions and the Staging of Sor Juana's *Los empeños de una casa*," Catherine Larson notes the large number of asides in the play, "Acts I and II have 19 apiece and Act III has an astonishing 38 asides; in addition, the servants have several scenes in which, alone onstage, they converse aloud, either in a monologue/soliloquy or by directly addressing the audience" (192). There are also remarks within speeches marked by parentheses that may also be interpreted and played as asides, such as the parenthetical comments in Ana's first long monologue. In addition, there are sections of long speeches that are not addressed to the other characters on stage, as when Rodrigo addresses an absent Leonor in his first scene with Hernando. If we include these remarks as asides and add soliloquies by Ana, Pedro, Juan, and others not mentioned by Larson, the number of asides and comments addressed to the audience becomes almost equal to the number of lines addressed to other characters.

As Larson notes, such heavy reliance on asides is common in *comedias de capa y espada* (cloak and sword plays) and in *comedias de enredo* (comedies of intrigue, a genre which describes *The House of Trials*). Sor Juana's use of these asides is typical when they reveal the thought processes of the characters and serve as moments of introspection. Her employment of asides becomes unique, however, when characters use them to reflect on the fact that they are characters in a play and to comment on the play and the playwright. The frequency and the patterns of the asides as well as their content emphasize the theatricality and self-reflectivity of *The House of Trials*. Sor

Juana uses asides, repetition, and self-referential remarks to remind the audience that they are watching a play that was written by a brilliant and talented nun.

The most typical use of asides in *The House of Trials* is for characters to explain what they are thinking, which reveals not only the thought process of the characters, but also how the characters interpret (or, as is so often the case, *mis*interpret) the plot complications and disguises. In the asides, the characters attempt to make sense of the confusion around them, and often make the plot even more complicated by jumping to conclusions and acting on those false conclusions as if they were true. Each character seems to be writing the action of the play in her or his asides, only to be frustrated by the plots created by the other characters in their asides.

Sor Juana uses asides so frequently that they begin to draw attention to themselves and become funny. The series of asides when Celia brings on the light in Act I, scene 3 illustrates this point:

> DOÑA LEONOR (*aside*): What is this? Heaven defend me! Isn't this Carlos I see?
> DON CARLOS (*aside*): Unless I'm deceived, this is Leonor!
> DOÑA ANA (*aside*): Don Juan here? I'm speechless!
> DON JUAN (*aside*): Why is Don Carlos here?

In performance, the audience begins laughing after either Ana's or Juan's line because the pattern calls attention to itself through repetition. The series of questions and exclamations creates a rhythm that drives the language forward, forcing the characters to behave and speak mechanically.

The creation of laughter through such repetition is discussed by theorist Henri Bergson in his famous essay *Laughter*, written in 1900. In this essay, which focuses mainly on Molière, Bergson noted that characters in plays are humorous when they behave in mechanical rather than organic ways, when they operate like rigid machines rather than flexible living organisms. Bergson described this comic technique as "the mechanical encrusted on the living" and applied it to the repetitious language patterns and actions of such characters as Orgon in *Tartuffe* and Harpagon in *The Miser*.

Sor Juana, who lived during the same time period as Molière, uses the same device not only in repetition of language patterns, but also in characterization. Juan becomes angry and draws his sword every time he sees Carlos. Rodrigo launches into a tirade about honor whenever he finds an opportunity to do so. Pedro repeatedly makes advances to Leonor who repeatedly rejects him. The pattern becomes so overwhelming for Pedro that he makes love to anyone who remotely looks like Leonor, including Castaño disguised in her clothing. Like characters in Molière or French farce, these men are funny because their behavior is so exaggerated and repetitive that it becomes mechanical and draws attention to itself.

In addition to individual characters behaving repetitiously, the overall action of the play contains the repeated device of characters misinterpreting what is happening around them. Juan mistakenly concludes Carlos must be Ana's lover, although Carlos really loves Leonor. Rodrigo mistakenly believes Pedro abducted Leonor, although Carlos was the man who eloped with her. Rodrigo also misinterprets why Carlos leaves Ana with him in the street and assumes that Carlos intended to elope with Ana. This last mistake causes Rodrigo to bring the woman he thinks is Ana (but who is really Leonor) to Pedro and to negotiate a marriage between Carlos and Ana. When Rodrigo informs Carlos that he has arranged for him to become "the fortunate owner of the beauty you adore," Carlos assumes Rodrigo means his daughter, Leonor. Carlos comments in an aside,

> What is this? Clearly,
> he knows what happened,
> so Castaño must have
> given him my letter [which reveals the truth].
> Knowing that I am the one who eloped with Leonor,
> Don Rodrigo wants to act
> fairly and give Leonor to me,

The audience laughs at his misreading of the situation, knowing the truth and realizing that Carlos' mistake is going to add another complication to an already very complicated plot fabricated out of a series of such misunderstandings.

The humor that Sor Juana creates in the series of misinterpretations is similar to the humor in the repetitive pattern of the asides. In both cases, the audience becomes aware of a mechanical pattern in the play. By calling attention to the artificiality of such patterns, Sor Juana makes the audience aware of the fact that they are watching a play and not real life, which is usually less formalized and more chaotic. In fact, the audience laughs partly out of self-consciousness at having been reminded that they are watching a play.

This self-awareness is reflected in the structure of the play itself. Some critics have accused the play of being "overly complicated," missing the point that the overabundance of complications is meant not only to be funny, but also to make the audience aware of the play's structure. The play as a whole can be seen as having a vastly complicated linear plot, but also as having a symmetrical structure. Act I begins with the exposition, then a street scene, then a scene in the dark, and then more complications. In Act III, the pattern moves in reverse: more complications, then a scene in the dark, then a street scene, then the denouement. Castaño's long monologue in Act III forms a structural parallel to Leonor's long monologue in Act I. The action of the last third of the play mirrors the action of the first third of the play.

At the center of the play, dividing the play in half, sits Ana's musical entertainment. The musical questions and answers serve as a performance within a performance, a play within a play. Each verse of the song reflects a pain of love which a particular character feels, thus commenting on the action of the play. The characters then comment on the musical entertainment, in a series of formal speeches with a rigid rhyme scheme. The characters call attention to the fact that they are in a play by critiquing a performance within the play and by doing so in speeches so highly structured that the structure calls attention to itself. After the serious speeches by Ana, Pedro, Leonor, and Carlos, the sequence ends with comic parodies of the device by Castaño and Celia. The repetitious nature of the structure calls attention to itself, and Sor Juana heightens the theatricality of the pattern by parodying it. Thus, Sor Juana uses the song, the four serious comments about the song, and the two comic parodies of the comments as mirrors within mirrors within mirrors: self-reflective parodies of self-reflective comments on a self-reflective song.

The self-reflective nature of the play's structure also appears in the play's metaphorical language. Throughout the play the comic servants have a series of puns in which one of the possible meanings of the words is theatrical. Celia calls Leonor's long speech a *relación*, which means both a flurry of activity and a stage monologue, and she continually refers to Ana's scheme as a *tramoya*, which means both a trick or deceit and a piece of stage machinery. Celia does this so often that it cannot be accidental; clearly Sor Juana intended these self-reflective remarks to call attention to the theatrical conventions of the play.

The clearest example of a character being aware that he is a character in a play occurs in Castaño's soliloquy in Act III while he is putting on Leonor's clothing. Not only does he call for a device worthy of the great playwright Pedro Calderón de la Barca, but he directly addresses the ladies in the audience early in the speech, refers later to one member of the audience as "Margaret," and calls another audience member "Your Excellency." (In common theatrical practice both in the seventeenth century and now, all asides and soliloquies are technically addressed to the audience in general, as if the audience were a social equal and friend of the character, but rarely are particular members of the audience addressed selectively as Castaño does here.) Throughout the play, and particularly in this soliloquy, Castaño is more aware of being a character in a play than any other character except Celia whose use of theatrical puns also reveals her awareness of being a character in a play. Their comic parodies of the comments on the song reflect this pattern of self-awareness in these two characters. The comic servants serve as the link between the reality of the play and the reality of the audience, repeatedly reminding the audience that they are watching a play.

Castaño's character is so aware of being a character that he remarks, "Please remember, ladies, that this is a play. Don't think that I hatched this scheme myself." Castaño implies that the plot device to which he refers was created by Sor Juana, since the original audience for whom the play was written knew the playwright personally and would have known that she had written the play. Sor Juana, then, calls attention not only to the fact that Castaño is a character in a play, but to the person who "hatched this scheme," namely herself.

Sor Juana sprinkles the dialogue with references to herself throughout the play. The most obvious example is Leonor's monologue in Act I about her intellect. The story about her fame adds little to the action of the play; its major purpose seems to be to remind the audience of Sor Juana's fame arising from her amazing intellect. Castaño's remark in Act III that someone else, not he, created the plot device emphasizes Sor Juana's ingenuity. In addition, references to nuns appear throughout the play: Celia jokingly suggests to Carlos that Leonor came to Pedro's room because she wanted to become a nun, Castaño compares being locked in the latticed room in Act II to being locked in a convent, and Leonor tells Celia in the last act that she wants to run away and hide from the world in a convent. The audience for whom this play was written knew that the playwright was a nun, so these remarks would serve to remind them of Sor Juana. Sor Juana repeatedly makes the audience aware of the intellect and profession of the authoress.

By giving the play a title, *Los empeños de una casa*, that mirrors one of Calderón's titles, *Los empeños de acasa* (*The Trials of Chance*), Sor Juana not only pays homage to Calderón, but also invites her audience to compare her play to those by Calderón. Castaño's reference to Calderón in Act III confirms Sor Juana's interest in reminding her audience of the great playwright. Through these devices, Sor Juana seeks to equate herself with the acknowledged master of the genre.

In *The Reply to Sister Philotea*, Sor Juana directly argues for the right of women to study, and in *The House of Trials*, she indirectly argues for the right of women to write plays. She calls attention to herself as playwright as a way of proving that women can write plays. She compares herself with Calderón to imply that if one woman can match wits with Calderón, then all women should be allowed the freedom and opportunity to do so. This idea was so radical in her time, that Sor Juana was forced to disguise it in humorous, self-reflective puns, allusions, and asides.

Feminist Interpretation of
The House of Trials

In her article entitled, "Sor Juana: Dream and Silence," Rachel Phillips states that Sor Juana Inés de la Cruz adopted the male models and male perspectives of the dominant culture in all of her writings except her autobiographical works *First Dream*, a philosophical poem about the search for knowledge, and *The Reply to Sister Philotea*, her treatise defending the right of women to study:

> In her plays she matched herself against Lope de Vega and Calderon, the earlier Spanish masters of the century. The results are flawlessly crafted works in which, as must have been her aim, the woman never shows, for she hides behind a male mask which is firm and rigid and lifeless. (35)

Sor Juana clearly modeled her comic masterpiece, *The House of Trials*, after Pedro Calderón de la Barca in terms of plot construction, character types, and poetic diction, but the result is not a "lifeless" imitation of Golden Age drama. As Electa Arenal points out in her article, "Sor Juana Inés de la Cruz: Speaking the Mother Tongue,"

> Sor Juana aimed unrelentingly at promoting respect for intelligence, at stimulating changes in the social relations between the sexes, and at publishing images of women as a powerful force in Catholicism, in history and culture. (99)

Sor Juana borrowed the conventions of Golden Age drama and then subverted them to suit her own proto-feminist views.

In her insightful article, "The Spanish Priest and the Mexican Nun: Two Views of Love and Honor", Patricia Kenworthy points out that, "Calderón's comedies typically begin with the problems of the men. . . . In contrast, *Los empeños de una casa* opens with the amorous adventures of the women" (106). This reversal of the traditional opening scene, emphasizing the female characters and their desires, suggests a shift from a male to a female perspective. Further evidence of this change occurs in the last act, when the comic servant directly addresses the audience. He speaks only to the women, although the audience for the premier performance apparently consisted of both men and women. Sor Juana's use of direct address to the women suggests that she might have been writing for a female audience, rather than for the "male gaze."

Stephanie Merrim, in her article "*Mores Geometricae*: The 'Womanscript' in the Theatre of Sor Juana Inés de la Cruz," proposes one of several possible feminist readings of *The House of Trials*. Merrim bases her interpretation on the critical theory of Sandra M. Gilbert and Susan Gubar in *The Madwoman in the Attic*. Merrim summarizes the theory, "We thus typically encounter in women's writings two competing heroines or polarized doubles, the angel and the monster, who may be understood as reflections of the writer's divided self" (100). Using this model, Merrim views Leonor as the angel of light, "Sor Juana's idealized mask" (105), and Ana as the creative woman whose fertile powers have no place in the rigid male society, and so she becomes the monster.

> Yet, most significant of all, the play has Ana manifest and put into action precisely that intelligence which is verbally imputed to Leonor (and shared by Sor Juana). In other words, the angel is imputed these qualities, but the monster enacts them. When Ana "directs" her play-within-a-play, Leonor is reduced to its passive victim, who at no point utilizes her alleged mental acuity to extricate herself from the labyrinth. Ana and Leonor, we see, are both *polarized*, into redeemed angel and punished creative monster, and covertly *equated* as the two halves of a divided self. (106)

In this reading of the play, Merrim interprets *The House of Trials* as a study of Sor Juana's inner torment and self-abasement:

> All told, nonetheless, one perceives in Sor Juana's works what has been described as a certain "melancholy," the melancholy of a woman who "soared above the rest" but never fully forgave herself her own daring, cognizant as she may have been of the "mistaken rules" that rendered her daring presumptuous. (119)

This feminist interpretation of *The House of Trials* converts a delightfully complex comic plot into a sad commentary on Sor Juana's psychological state and her conflicted emotions about being an intelligent and creative woman in a male-dominated society.

Merrim's reading of the text sets Ana on centerstage and displaces Leonor, making Ana the protagonist and Leonor the passive victim. It is possible, however, to discover a feminist interpretation of *The House of Trials* with Leonor as a feminist heroine and Ana as the supporter of the patriarchy. Constance Wilkins argues for this interpretation in "Subversion through Comedy? Two Plays by Sor Juana Inés de la Cruz and María de Zayas." In Wilkins' analysis of the play, Leonor rejects the patriarchal world of her father by leaving his house with a foreigner, Carlos. "Leonor is successful in challenging the usual sources of power and, by achieving her desired outcome, she has a voice in shaping her world" (114). Wilkins sees Leonor as the catalyst who initiates the action of the play and the center of the new society formed at the end. Whereas Merrim views Leonor as a passive victim who, despite her intellect, plays the traditional feminine role, Wilkins perceives Leonor as an active agent of rebellion and social change.

Wilkins also argues that Sor Juana transformed Calderón's conceptions of love and honor as she borrowed them. She claims Sor Juana imitates

> Calderón's treatment of honor precisely to show its defects. Throughout the play, Ana uses the rules of the conventional code of honor to deceive and manipulate others. (116)

In consenting to participate in the plan of her male guardian, Pedro, Ana begins by accepting a patriarch's view of the world (in opposition to Leonor who begins by rejecting patriarchal authority). She manipulates Carlos by pretending to fear the loss of her honor and deceives Leonor by feigning concern for Leonor's honor. This use of honor as a shield for dishonorable love reveals the hypocrisy inherent in the Spanish code of honor.

Just as Sor Juana borrows Calderón's code of honor only to discredit it, so she takes the gender stereotypes inherited from Calderón only to satirize traditional male and female behavior. Kenworthy notes that tension in Calderón's comic action arises from the conflict between the opposing male and female sensibilities, "between the outer world of masculine action, order, and arms and the inner world of feminine imagination and eroticism . . ." (107). The male represents the outside world, reason, honor, and physical action, while the female represents the domestic sphere, desire, danger, and deceit. Heroes fight to achieve their orderly and honorable goals through duels, while heroines scheme to satisfy their passions through "feminine wiles." Calderón's *La dama duende* (*The Phantom Lady*) with its clever heroine who uses intrigue to defeat her rigid, honor-obsessed brother exemplifies this dichotomy of male and female roles.

Sor Juana employed this dichotomy in *The House of Trials* in her characterization of the brother and sister who live in the house mentioned in the title, Pedro and Ana. Unlike Calderón's brother-sister pairs who operate in opposition to one another (as in *The Phantom Lady*), these two work as a team, but the roles assigned to each reflect Calderón's conception of male and female psychology. Pedro, as the man of action, acts outside the home, taking Leonor from Carlos at sword point and kidnapping her. Once he brings her to his house, Ana takes over in the domestic sphere and creates what Merrim calls "an enchanted labyrinth" (104). She uses deceit, half-truths, outright lies, and a Baroque musical performance in her attempts to divide Carlos and Leonor. Ana's schemes put Carlos and Leonor into situations in which "the characters can see but not hear, while in others, they can hear but not see, leaving them in a state of sensory unawareness" (Larson 189). Pedro performs in the public sphere and, although not completely honest with Leonor about his role in her abduction, is at least honest about his desire to marry her, while Ana acts in the privacy of the home, continually devising lies and scheming to deceive Carlos and Leonor, plying her "feminine wiles" on them.

Despite the fact that Pedro and Ana behave in culturally appropriate ways, they are the villains of *The House of Trials*. They plot to separate the true lovers, Carlos and Leonor, who undergo trials of their love in Pedro and Ana's house. Although Pedro and Ana embody the dominant society's gender roles, they fail to achieve their desires.

The plot devised by Ana and Pedro depends on Leonor and Carlos adhering to traditional gender stereotypes. Sor Juana, however, created two atypical characters in Leonor and Carlos. Both her heroine and her hero exhibit qualities traditionally assigned to the opposite gender. The androgynous personalities of Leonor and Carlos defeat Ana's and Pedro's plan precisely because they mix stereotypically masculine and feminine traits.

Leonor's androgyny derives from mixing feminine beauty with "masculine" reason. Both Ana and Celia immediately notice and comment on Leonor's extraordinary feminine beauty, but Leonor, in her long Act One monologue, emphasizes her intellect, noting how her mental powers amazed the masculine culture which assumed that women's intellect had to be inferior to men's. Leonor's genius would not have created this frenzy if she were a man. In this way, Sor Juana commented on her society's insistence on distinct gender roles and revealed some of the problems encountered by those, like herself, who did not adhere to those limitations.

Rather than being neutered by this combination, Leonor retains the positive attributes of both genders. Although she threatens to pine away in a convent at one point, Leonor usually remains temperate and reasonable, at least more reasonable than Ana, the embodiment of the typical jealous and wily Spanish heroine. Leonor's even temperament and ability to reason leads her through the deceits created by Ana, without lowering herself to Ana's level and indulging in deceit. By refusing to play the traditional role of the wily schemer, Leonor triumphs in the end by marrying Carlos.

Sor Juana created the perfect androgynous mate for Leonor in Carlos. Leonor's description of him in the first act emphasizes his combination of "manly strength and feminine beauty." Leonor comments that Carlos' beauty is dangerous, because it caused her to disobey her father and elope with him. She also notes his "gentle grace" and his "meekness," which are traditionally feminine attributes. In other words, she first fell in love with him for his "feminine" qualities. Along with his delicacy of feeling and charming manners, Leonor also observes his daring spirit, valiant courage, and subtle intellect, which are traditionally masculine attributes. This paradox combines qualities that the period considered feminine (gentleness, charm, and humility) with qualities considered masculine (daring, physical action, and reason). Inwardly and outwardly, Carlos appears androgynous to Leonor and that is why she loves him.

This androgyny gives Carlos an advantage over the more stereotypically masculine men in the play. In spite of all of Ana's trickery, Carlos questions his senses and his sanity before he questions Leonor's virtue or her devotion to him. He assumes, despite all evidence to the contrary, that Leonor would not betray him. Lacking Pedro's blind instinct for immediate swordplay, Carlos thinks before he acts and refuses to be deceived by appearances. His gentleness and delicacy of feeling, that is, his feminine aspects, protect him against the traps arranged by Pedro, Ana, and their maid.

Androgyny not only draws Leonor and Carlos to one another, but it allows them to escape the petty jealousies and fits of rage that characterize the other women and men. They are the only pair of lovers who achieve their desire. They triumph over the scheming of Pedro and Ana, because they avoid the extremes of "masculine" anger and "feminine" jealousy. In the words of Wilkins, "because of their unswerving devotion, Leonor and Carlos ultimately determine the outcome and may represent a utopian dream of female-male integration" (110-1). Clearly, Sor Juana viewed them as ideal, both as individuals and as a couple, because of their androgyny.

Ana and Juan form the other romantic couple in *The House of Trials*. Juan behaves with stereotypical masculinity as Ana acts with stereotypical femininity. Just as Pedro bribed Leonor's maid to discover her planned elopement with Carlos, Juan bribed Celia to gain entry into the house. Like Pedro, Juan indulges in physical force rather than persuasion and attempts to rape Ana. He "reasons" that he deserves to take Ana by force since she behaved so cruelly. "Masculine" reason leads him to a masculine show of physical force. His perversion of logic and instinct for physical action lead him to attempt to destroy honor rather than to preserve it. Through the character of Juan, Sor Juana showed that reason and action do not necessarily lead to honor and that men are not inherently more reasonable or honorable than women.

In addition, Sor Juana used the characters of Juan, Pedro, and Rodrigo to satirize the culture's objectification of women.

Rodrigo and Pedro, with Juan serving as the broker, negotiate a forced marriage between Pedro and Leonor like a business deal, never thinking of consulting with Leonor. Rodrigo claims:

> It does not matter
> whether Leonor agrees or not
> to what you have proposed,
> since nothing could please her more
> than obeying my commands.
> So call her, and you will see
> how quickly the bargain is settled.

Although they act in accordance with the strict Spanish honor code, these men appear self-centered and callous towards women, revealing the misogyny inherent in that code. In the next act, Rodrigo and Pedro negotiate a marriage between Ana and Carlos with equal insensitivity to true love and the woman's preference. To achieve the appearance of honor, they sacrifice both the truth of what happened and the feelings of the women.

Sor Juana highlighted this objectification of women by demonstrating how interchangeable the women are to these men. In the first act, Juan grabs Leonor in the dark, mistaking her for Ana and tries to rape her. Leonor, of course, runs away, and tells him that he obviously has mistaken her for someone else. Using her reason, Leonor quickly realizes the truth of the situation. Juan, however, does not listen to her words or realize that it is not Ana's voice. He cannot differentiate among the women in the dark. In the last act, Pedro courts a servant dressed in Leonor's clothes. Although Pedro notices that this person uses vulgar words and expressions uncharacteristic of Leonor, he fails to observe that the voice is not hers. As Juan cannot recognize women in the dark, so Pedro cannot differentiate among people in veils. Women remain mysterious objects to these men, bodies to be entered by force, commodities to be negotiated, or prizes to be sought in marriage.

Sor Juana created a unique punishment for Pedro's objectification. The veiled object of his affection in the last act is not really a woman, but Carlos' comic servant, Castaño. In having Castaño disguise himself in Leonor's clothing, Sor Juana created the most obvious image of androgyny in *The House of Trials*. As he dons Leonor's clothes, Castaño transforms himself into his own ideal of femininity. Wilkins notes, "The fool in drag preens before the audience, commenting on his appearance and charms, and makes fun of young men who love not beauty but what they think beauty is" (112). Sor Juana used Castaño's disguise to comment on the male ideal of a beautiful woman and on male vanity.

Sor Juana revealed the fallibility of traditional male assumptions in Pedro's reaction to the disguise. Unlike Carlos, Pedro falls prey to appearances and assumes that the veiled figure before him is Leonor (in spite of Castaño's crude language and vulgar insults) and makes arrangements to marry him/her, unaware of the homosexual implications. In the end, "Pedro receives the most severe punishment allowed by *comedia* norms, remaining unmarried" (Merrim 103–4).

The device of a man disguising himself in woman's clothing is not unique to Sor Juana, although Electa Arenal claims, "Thus she created the only male character in Hispanic comedy who disguises himself as a woman . . ." (101). Male characters in drag are rare in Spanish Golden Age drama, far more rare than female characters in male dress which is relatively common. Lope de Vega, Calderón, Ruiz de Alarcón, and Tirso de Molina all use the device at least once, but Sor Juana exploits the comic possibilities of drag better than any of these men.

Even when creating female characters who dressed as men, Hispanic playwrights did not experiment with gender ambiguity as Shakespeare does in *Twelfth Night* or Sor Juana does in *The House of Trials*. Sor Juana, like Shakespeare, explores the attractiveness of androgyny. The audience watches one man make love to another, fully aware of the irony, and the possibility of a homosexual union is raised. With her interest in androgyny and sexual ambiguity, Sor Juana traveled through territory uncharted in Spanish drama before her.

The homosexual union never actually happens, of course; the rigid Catholicism of the period would not permit it. Instead, Castaño, who lustily and rudely pursued Celia in Act Two, asks her to marry him in the last lines of the play. Although the marriage of servants is traditional at the end of Golden Age *comedia*, this event could be interpreted as evidence that Castaño has learned to understand and appreciate women better for having experienced a little of what they commonly encounter. Instead of crudely suggesting a quick tumble together, he respects Celia enough to make a commitment to her. Masquerading as a women, exploring his feminine side, has him a better man. Castaño, like Carlos and Leonor, is rewarded for being androgynous.

The stereotypically feminine Ana must resign herself to marrying a violent man she no longer loves, and the stereotypically masculine Juan blindly blunders into a life-long commitment to a woman who no longer loves him. Sor Juana punished conformity to these gender roles by forcing them into a stereotypical marriage, as if the crime of adhering to rigid, traditional roles contained its own poetic justice.

By extolling androgyny and mocking gender stereotypes, Sor Juana's *The House of Trials* challenged the dominant male culture in seventeenth-century New Spain. Through seemingly minor variations on Calderón's dramaturgy, she radically altered his male viewpoint and promoted a feminist perspective. As Julie Greer Johnson notes in *Women in Colonial Spanish America: Literary Images*:

> While Sor Juana relies upon stereotypes and dramatic convention, these technical recourses afford her the opportunity of registering her discontent on several issues regarding women without appearing to break with tradition. The pressures of a strict, unyielding society that neither anticipated nor fully accepted the emergence of such a gifted woman made the use of these artifices imperative. (129)

Sor Juana worked within the poetic and dramatic traditions of the Golden Age because she was probably commissioned to do so, but by subverting the conventions of Calderón she created both a popular comedy and a subtle criticism of the treatment of women in her time.

Bibliography

I. Editions used in preparing the translation:
García Valdés, Celsa Carmen, ed. *Los empeños de una casa* by Sor Juana Inés de la Cruz. Barcelona: Promociones y Publicaciones Universitarias, S. A., 1989.

Salceda, Alberto G. *Obras completas de Sor Juana Inés de la Cruz*, volume 4. Mexico: Fondo de Cultura Económica, 1957.

II. General books and articles on Sor Juana in English:
Arenal, Electa. "Comment on Paz's 'Juana Ramírez'." *Signs* 5.3 (Spring 1980): 552-5.

———. "The Convent as Catalyst for Autonomy." *Women in Hispanic Literature: Icons and Fallen Idols*. Beth Miller ed. Berkeley: University of California Press, 1983.

———. "Sor Juana Inés de la Cruz: Speaking the Mother Tongue." *University of Dayton Review* 16.2 (Spring 1983): 93-105.

———. "This Life Within Me Won't Keep Still." *Reinventing the Americas*. Bell Gale Chevigny and Gari Laguardia, eds. New York: Cambridge University Press, 1986.

Burke, Marcus. [untitled article on a portrait of Sor Juana Inés de la Cruz attributed to Juan de Miranda]. *Mexico. Splendors of Thirty Centuries*. Boston: Bulfinch Press, 1990.

Flynn, Gerard. *Sor Juana Inés de la Cruz*. New York: Twayne Publishers, Inc., 1971.

———. "Sor Juana Inés de la Cruz: Mexico's Tenth Muse." *Female Scholars: A Tradition of Learned Women before 1800*. J. R. Brink, ed. Montreal: Eden Press Women's Publications, 1980.

Johnson, Julie Greer. *Women in Colonial Spanish American Literature: Literary Images.* Westport, Conn.: Greenwood Press, 1983.

Merrim, Stephanie, ed. *Feminist Perspectives on Sor Juana Inés de la Cruz.* Detroit: Wayne State University Press, 1991.

Myles, Eileen. "Nun's Tale: The Selling of Sor Juana." *The Village Voice Literary Supplement* 75 (June 1989): 30–31.

Paz, Octavio. *Sor Juana, or, The Traps of Faith.* Trans. Margaret Sayers Peden. Cambridge, Mass.: Harvard University Press, 1988.

Phillips, Rachel. "Sor Juana: Dream and Silence." *Aphra* 3.1 (Winter 1971-2): 30–40.

Royer, Fanchón. *The Tenth Muse: Sor Juana Inés de la Cruz.* Peterson, N.J.: St. Anthony Guild Press, 1952.

Schons, Dorothy. "Some Bibliographical Notes on Sor Juana Inés de la Cruz." *University of Texas Bulletin* 2526 (July 8, 1925): 1–30.

———. "Some Obscure Points in the Life of Sor Juana Inés de la Cruz." *Modern Philology* 24.2 (Nov. 1926): 141–162.

Terry, Arthur. "The Tenth Muse: Recent Work on Sor Juana Inés de la Cruz." *Bulletin of Hispanic Studies* 66.2 (April 1989): 161– 6.

Thurman, Judith. "Sister Juana: The Price of Genius." *Ms.* 1.10 (April 1973): 14–21.

Trueblood, Alan S. *A Sor Juana Anthology.* Cambridge, Mass.: Harvard University Press, 1988.

Williamsen, Vern G. *The Minor Dramatists of Seventeenth-Century Spain.* Boston: Twayne Publishers, 1982.

III. Articles on *The House of Trials* in English:

Kenworthy, Patricia. "The Spanish Priest and the Mexican Nun: Two Views of Love and Honor." *Calderón de la Barca at the*

Tercentenary: Comparative Views. Wendell M. Aycock and Sydney P. Cravens, eds. Lubbock, Texas: Texas Tech Press, 1982.

Larson, Catherine. "Writing the Performance: Stage Directions and the Staging of Sor Juana's *Los empeños de una casa.*" *Bulletin of the Comediantes* 42.2 (Winter 1990): 179-198.

Merrim, Stephanie. "*Mores Geometricae*: The 'Womanscript' in the Theater of Sor Juana Inés de la Cruz." *Feminist Perspectives on Sor Juana Inés de la Cruz.* Stephanie Merrim, ed. Detroit: Wayne State University Press, 1991.

Pasquariello, Anthony M. "The Seventeenth-Century Interlude in the New World Secular Theater." *Homage to Irving A. Leonard.* Raquel Chang-Rodríquez and Donald A. Yates, eds. Lansing, Mich.: Latin American Studies Center, Michigan State University, 1977.

Pasto, David. "Sor Juana's Subversion of Gender Stereotypes in *Los empeños de una casa.*" *Women in Theatre: The Journal for the Women in Theatre Interdisciplinary Conference.* New York: Greenwood Press, anticipated 1997.

Wilkins, Constance. "Subversion through Comedy? Two Plays by Sor Juana Inés de la Cruz and María de Zayas." The Perception of Women in Spanish Theater of the *Golden Age.* Anita K. Stoll and Dawn L. Smith, eds. Lewisburg, Penn.: Bucknell University Press, 1991.

IV. Translations of other works by Sor Juana:

Flores, Angel and Kate Flores, eds. *The Defiant Muse: Hispanic Feminist Poems from the Middle Ages to the Present.* New York: The Feminist Press, 1986.

Peden, Margaret Sayers. *A Woman of Genius: The Intellectual Autobiography of Sor Juana Inés de la Cruz.* Salisbury, Conn.: Lime Rock Press, Inc., 1982.

Trueblood, Alan S. *A Sor Juana Anthology.* Cambridge, Mass.: Harvard University Press, 1988.

Warnke, Frank J. *Three Women Poets: Renaissance and Baroque: Louise Labe, Gaspara Stampa, Sor Juana Inés de la Cruz.* Lewisburg, Penn.: Bucknell University Press, 1987.

The House of Trials[1]

by Sor Juana Inés de la Cruz
translated by David J. Pasto

Dramatis personae in order of appearance:

DOÑA ANA, sister of Pedro
CELIA, her maid
DOÑA LEONOR, in love with Carlos
DON CARLOS, in love with Leonor
CASTAÑO[2], his servant
DON RODRIGO, father of Leonor
HERNANDO, his servant
DON JUAN, in love with Ana
DON PEDRO, brother of Ana
Two masked men
Singers and Musicians

The action takes place in and around the house where Ana and Pedro live in Toledo, Spain.

This translation premiered at Oklahoma City University on April 20, 1995.

The Cast (in order of appearance):

Celia, Ana's maid	Sarah Pfeiffer
Don Juan, in love with Ana	Josh White
Doña Ana, Pedro's sister	Gianna L. Fregosi
Masked Man, disguised as the police	Jerry Rucker, Jr.
Doña Leonor, in love with Carlos	Selina McNeel
Don Carlos, in love with Leonor	Timothy Goins
Don Diego, Leonor's cousin[3]	Michael Lopez
Don Pedro, Ana's sister	Trey Irby
Castaño, Carlos' servant	John Fletcher
Don Rodrigo, Leonor's father	Hal Greenwood
Hernanda[4]	Lisa Daniels
Guitarist and Music Arranger	Michael Fersonke
Singers	E. Cherelle Hale and Jerry Rucker, Jr.

The Production Staff

Director	David Pasto
Costume Designer	Billie Boston
Scene Designer	James A. Stuhlmiller
Lighting Designer	Robert L. Lawrence
Fight Choreographer	Don Lebermann

The premiere production was revived at Oklahoma City University in March 1996 because it was invited to perform at the twenty-first annual International *Siglo de Oro* Theatre Festival in El Paso, Texas, on March 6, 1996.

The Association for Hispanic Classical Theatre granted the production the Walter M. Reid Award to help defray the cost of traveling to the festival and granted the translator the Franklin G. Smith Award for excellence in translation.

The Cast for the Festival (in order of appearance):

Celia, Ana's maid	Jolie Beth Boudreaux
Don Juan, in love with Ana	Scott Hale
Doña Ana, Pedro's sister	Elizabeth Fletcher
Masked Man, disguised as the police	Daniel C. Webb
Doña Leonor, in love with Carlos	Selina McNeel
Don Carlos, in love with Leonor	Timothy Goins
Don Diego, Leonor's cousin	Michael Lopez
Don Pedro, Ana's sister	Trey Irby
Castaño, Carlos' servant	John Fletcher
Don Rodrigo, Leonor's father	Hal Greenwood
Hernanda	Elizabeth Inghram
Guitarist and Music Arranger	Michael Fersonke
Singers	Elizabeth Inghram and Daniel C. Webb

ACT ONE

SCENE ONE

[IN THE HOUSE, LATE AT NIGHT.]

(*DOÑA ANA and CELIA enter.*)[5]

DOÑA ANA: We must wait up, Celia,
until my brother arrives.

CELIA: I'll keep an eye out for him.
He'll be late, because he thinks
    one or two in the morning is early.
It's best to speak the truth,
even though it's obvious:
He won't come until morning.
    But what makes you
so impatient now?
Why don't you go to bed as usual
and I'll wait for him alone?

DOÑA ANA: You must know, Celia,
my brother has placed all his trust in me,
such is his confidence
in my affection for him.
    As you well know, he left
Madrid two years ago,
and came here to Toledo,
to settle a debt.
    Expecting to return soon,
he left me in Madrid
where I remained unprotected,[6]
able to be seen and to see.
    Don Juan saw me and I saw him.
He courted me lovingly,
and I responded
to his faithful heart.
    Then, either because the dispute
wasn't as simple as he thought

or in fact because
my brother didn't want to leave—
    because here lives a lady
so beautiful
that words fail
to adequately praise her fame.
    He fell in love with her,
And, because she didn't return his love,
the lost soul stayed in Toledo
in order to win her.
    So either because I was
unprotected in Madrid without him
or because he sought relief
from his cruel love,
    he arranged for me to come
live with him. Immediately,
I sent word to Don Juan, who followed me
like a faithful lover to Toledo.
    I should have been grateful
for this gallantry with all my soul.
If only, alas!, I did not repent
the entire affair,
    because Love, which is
lustful and crude at heart,
offends nobility.[7]
But, returning to my brother;
    you should know that he inquired
with stubborn determination
the reason why he wasn't able
to win her love.
    He discovered she loves another man,
although I don't know who he is.
He felt more despised
since she favored another,
    and devised a desperate plan,
since the poison of jealousy
makes one feel another's gain
more than one's own injury.
    He was so desperate
and in such a state that

he bribed
her trusted maid.
    (Oh, vile custom!
that reason is so ruined,
that love is so blind,
that it pays to bring grief!)
    He learned from
the unfaithful maid
that the lady had planned
to steal away from her house
    with her lover tonight.
That made my brother furious,
and such jealous men
will risk any danger.
    He arranged with some men
to pretend to be the police
(see how cunning evil can be!)
who'd arrest the man who stole his love.
    As the men passed by
with the lover and the beautiful lady,
they were to leave her with me,
trusting me to keep her safe.
    Then, they'd leave with the lover
and pretend to be careless,
giving him
a chance to escape.
    The idea being that
he'd run away
thinking that he'd
escaped from the police.
    My brother, with this scheme
devised by his love,
would have his lady brought
to his house without risk.
    It will be easy for him
to woo her passionately
without him seeming to be guilty
or her being able to object.
    If she learned of his scheme,
she'd be enraged.

        Obviously, she'd hate
anyone who'd abused her like that.
        Because of what I've told you,
Celia, I must wait up.
You see, how could I go to bed
and sleep peacefully?

CELIA: Señora[8], nothing surprises me.
It's common for lovers
to hide the truth
in the guise of a lie.
        Who'd be shocked
if they happened to hear about
the foolishness of a woman,
the determination of a lover,
        or the treachery of a maid?
These things happen all the time.
Isn't there such a cauldron of troubles
boiling in this house?
        The only thing that's surprised me
is your behavior.
It seems that your heart
has forgotten Don Juan.
        I don't know why you're trying
so hard to forget him
when you've no reason for it.
Don Juan gives you no cause for complaint.

DOÑA ANA: He gives me no cause, that's true;
but I have my reasons.

CELIA: Which are?

DOÑA ANA: Are you surprised?
The will is blind.
        Don Juan, as you know,
followed me lovingly and gallantly.
As I withdrew from him,
he became more passionate,
        suffocating

my free-will.
Since I'd won him so easily,
I lost interest in him.[9]
　　But that's not the only
reason for my coldness:
for another fire
has purged him from my heart.
　　In the street, I saw
a handsome young man pass by.
If he's not Apollo[10] himself,
I don't know who he could be.
　　Alas, Celia! I don't know
if this is a whim or a fantasy,
and . . . But I've said this
without knowing what I was saying.

CELIA: Are you crying?

DOÑA ANA: 　　　　Why shouldn't I cry,
unfaithful me!, when
I know that I'm wrong
but I can't correct myself?

CELIA (*aside*): It's a good thing
I heard about this now,
because I've hidden
Don Juan in her room.
　　Noticing the way
she treated him with scorn,
he wants to take her by force,[11]
and ruin everything.
(*aloud*) 　　Señora, who's won
your love?

DOÑA ANA: 　　　I can only say
that the young man is
Don Carlos de Olmedo.
　　But someone's knocking.
See who it is, Celia,
then I'll talk to you later.

CELIA: Who is it?

A MASKED MAN (*off-stage*): The police!

DOÑA ANA: It's the lady:
    open the door, Celia.

CELIA: Come in.

(*TWO MASKED MEN enter with DOÑA LEONOR*)[12]

A MASKED MAN: Señora Doña Ana, I'm not ignorant
    of the honor of this family,
    and I believe I entered this house
    more out of respect
    than in offense. And so, I beg
    you to take this lady
    I entrust to you, while
    they investigate the case of
    the man who was with her,
    who killed another man.
    Forgive me, I must return
    to my duties.

(*THE MASKED MEN exit.*)

DOÑA ANA: What is this?
    Celia, call back those men
    who brought this woman.
    I'm not accustomed
    to meeting such loose women.

CELIA (*aside*): How well my mistress
    pretends not to want her.

DOÑA LEONOR: Señora, (my heart is in my mouth)
    Poor me! If my tender tears
    can move you to pity
    (I'm not saying this right),

I beg you on my knees
to take pity on my reputation,
if not on my life.
Since I entered your house,
don't allow them to take me to another
where my reputation
would be ruined. If I were
a loose woman as you imagine,
I wouldn't have made this plea to you
nor would I have such anxieties.

DOÑA ANA (*aside to CELIA*):   Her beauty and her shame
have moved me to tears.
My brother described her well, Celia.

CELIA (*aside to DOÑA ANA*):   Her beauty is superhuman.
And if it's so in raining tears,
how must it be in fair weather?

DOÑA ANA (*aloud*):   Stand up, Señora,
and pardon me if, confused
by the suddenness of the event,
I showed a lack of
courtesy and respect.
Ignorance of who you are
explains my discourtesy.
But already your wounded person
speaks in your favor,
so with all my soul
I promise to help you.

DOÑA LEONOR: Allow me to kneel at your feet,
beautiful goddess, whose temple,
whose shrine, whose altar,
is the sanctuary
of my misfortune.

DOÑA ANA: Stand up,
and tell me what could have
caused such unhappiness.

Although such beauty,
often brings misery.

CELIA (*aside*): Thank God, I'm free
of the envy she feels!

DOÑA LEONOR: Señora, although shame
could prevent me
from telling the story
of how I happen to be
in this miserable condition,
I can't keep silent.
Instead, I think it's better
to do as you command,
because it appears that
I must be guilty of some crime.
The causes are more honest
than they appear to be.
Hear me out.

DOÑA ANA: I will
listen quietly.

CELIA: That's great!
A monologue[13] in the middle of the night
by candlelight? God forbid!

DOÑA LEONOR: Listen, if you want to hear
the sad circumstances of my story,
which reveal the depths of my misfortune.
They may interest you,
for hearing of my troubles
may put you at ease;
and by expressing my grief,
I may find relief
for the pain I feel
by recounting my sorrows.
   I was nobly born; and
this was the beginning of my troubles,
because it's no small misfortune

to be noble but poor.
Although nobility is a jewel
of great value,
it's also a gaudy ornament,
which only served to embarrass me,
by subjecting me to
the opposing contradictions
between poverty
and aristocratic pretensions.
   I assume there is no need
to mention that I was born beautiful,
since your eyes witness it,
and my troubles prove it.
I only say—and I'd rather not
be the one to say it,
because I see reasons both
for keeping silent
and for speaking out—
I say that I was
famous for my amazing intellect.
The need to say so,
makes me sound as if I'm lying,
but if I don't say it,
I'm not speaking the truth.
It sounds foolish to speak of
my intellect in telling my story
(although my modesty must suffer
the shame of telling it)
but in order to understand my life,
you must realize
that my intellect was
the principle cause of my downfall.[14]
   From my early childhood,
I was inclined to study
with such burning zeal,
with such eager concern,
that I learned much
in a short space of time.
With the intensity and diligence
of my studying, time passed quickly,

and soon I was
the target of admiration,
noticed by everyone,
who then came
to worship my acquired laurels
as a sign of divine grace.
Throughout my native land,
I was worshipped
with the kind of adoration
created by popular acclaim.
Whatever I said,
right or wrong,
was enhanced by my face
and given authority by my appearance.
Popular superstition
reached such a frenzy
that they worshipped as a deity
the idol they'd created.[15]

    My fame flew like gossip,
spreading into foreign countries,
and exaggerated tales were believed
in distant lands.
My modest accomplishments
were blown out of proportion,
as if distorted
by a magnifying lens.
Bowed down in devotion
like sacrifices at my altar,
the hearts of everyone
were at once universally ensnared
in a spontaneous cult.
The cult became the fashion,
practiced by everyone,
being an obligatory
ritual at court.
And if someone foolishly
or wisely objected,
they did not dare to say so,
fearing their unpopular opinion,
being in the minority,

would be considered
an indication of bad manners
or the censure of jealousy.
    Amid this applause,
capsizing in the attentions
of the multitudes,
I could find no safe harbor.
Being loved by everyone,
I found no one to love.
Fearlessly against the crowds
I defended my virtue
from the greatest of dangers
and the worst of harms.
Balancing affectionate attention
with courteous modesty,
I usually avoided
suspicious intentions.
My parents, vainly trusting
in my measured countenance,
did nothing to protect me.
What a mistake
it was to remove
the guards and the locks
from someone so buffeted
with contradictory forces!
And as they were
foolishly careless with me,
I fell precisely into the danger
they allowed to happen.
    It happened, then, that
amid those incited by my fame
who came to confirm it in my person,
there came to see me by chance
(Oh God, how could you permit
such a tyrannical passion
to forge itself by chance!),
a young stranger named
Don Carlos de Olmedo.
He's so illustrious by birth
that wherever he chooses to lodge,

although he's not famous,
he cannot be ignored.[16]
    Here I take the license
you offer me to describe him,
in order to explain my downfall
and to express my anxieties.
Don't be surprised at
the bold extremity
of my love, which
merits such attention.
His face was an enigma,
composed of two contradictions—
manly strength and feminine beauty—
so fortuitously harmonized
that his beauty,
lacking softness,
found the greatest perfection
in what it most lacked.
His features were marred
with a masculine boldness,
which did not allow beauty
to have imperial sway.
His beauty was
so far from his attention,
so alien to his awareness,
that he did not notice it.
Such an overabundance
of beauty in a man
is wonderful to own,
but distasteful when displayed.
    Although Nature
might contrive to give another
such a form as his,
such manners and such grace,
could only suit
Carlos' soul.
Providence formed
him perfectly
uniting so gentle a form
with so daring a spirit.

He enjoyed an intellect
so subtle, so sublime,
that he was wise
beyond his years.
The heart of these perfections
was the gentle grace
of such lively energy,
of such pleasing manners,
of such amiable modesty,
of such attractive affability,
that in the slightest gesture
one found the greatest beauty.
So humble in his affections,
so tender in his attentions,
so polished in his pleadings,
so meek in his manners,
and so perfect in every way,
he courteously displayed
the refinements of the devoted
with the nobility of the valiant.
He endured my disdain and
kept silent about my favors.
Determining the dangers,
he prudently took his chances.
You see that these endowments,
along with others I haven't mentioned,
would defeat the defenses
of the most sensible and virtuous woman.
     Finally, I fell in love with him.
I don't want to bore you
by giving a moment by moment account
of my reckless trials,
since you must know
about the trials of love,
customarily beginning
with restlessness and anxiety,
leading to dangers and risks,
and ending in grievances or tragedies.
Love grew in both of us
equally, and we longed

to celebrate our happy union
in a chaste bridal bed,
confirmed by the eternal bond
of marriage.[17]
My father, in order
to find me a husband,
was already measuring and comparing
the merits of my suitors.
So while he was attending to other affairs
and would not hinder us,
we arranged to elope
tonight. Trampling on
the affections of my father
and the reputation of my honor,
I entered the street, and
as soon as I took the first steps,
I felt a fearful foreboding
of my misfortune. I clutched
my skirt with one hand
and my veil with the other,
when two masked men suddenly
approached us.
"Who goes there?" they said, and I
with a trembling voice
without thinking about what I was doing
(for in such cases
the care one takes to keep secrets
causes one to reveal them)
I said, "Ah, Carlos, we are lost."
And as soon as my words
reached their ears,
the two men drew their swords;
and one of them said,
"I'll kill him.[18]
This woman he is kidnapping
is my cousin, Doña Leonor de Castro."
My lover drew his sword
and immediately struck a blow
with the point of his sword
at the heart of his opponent.

He cried out and fell to the ground.
Seeing the calamity,
he called to his companion,
and at his command
some men appeared.
Although Carlos could have fled,
he wouldn't leave me.
He bravely stayed on
until the police,
who were making their rounds,
approached us.
Although he was prepared
to defend himself again,
persuaded by my tears,
he yielded his sword to my entreaties
rather than to his enemies.
    In short, they arrested him
and me as an accessory to the crime,
for the man he killed was my cousin,
Don Diego de Castro.
    They deposited
my person and my misfortunes
in your noble house, Señora,
where suddenly I find myself
without reputation, without honor,
without consolation, without relief,
without courage, without comfort;
only waiting for
the execution of my death
with Carlos' death sentence.

DOÑA ANA (*aside*):   Oh God! What's this I hear?
    The same man I idolize
    is in love with Leonor.
    Oh, how quickly Don Juan's love
    is avenged! How unfortunate!
(*aloud*)   Señora, I sympathize
    with your honorable concerns.
    Celia, take this lady to my room,
    while I wait for my brother.

CELIA: Come, Señora.

DOÑA LEONOR: I'll follow you
as, unfortunately, I must
follow my fate.

(*CELIA and DOÑA LEONOR exit.*)

DOÑA ANA: Since the grace and gallantry of Carlos[19]
had enough power to make me love him,
how will they appear now
that jealousy adds to the attraction?
If I tried in vain to win his love,
knowing that he loves another,
what would I gain by keeping him
apart from his first love?
Pardon me, Don Juan. Although I want
to return your love and condemn my neglect,
how could I, now that jealousy
has thrust its poison into my suffering?
Carlos is the most handsome suitor,[20]
but his suit belongs to another.

(*DON CARLOS enters with his sword drawn along with CASTAÑO.*)

DON CARLOS: Señora, if misfortunes can find
sanctuary in your mercy,
show your great mercy
in offering sanctuary to mine.
Just behind me is
no less than the police.
Although fleeing from them
is an honorable retreat,[21]
my persecuted spirit
asks sanctuary for my body,
although my life means little to me,
since I have lost my soul.

CASTAÑO: My life means a lot to me,

Señora, so fearfully
I beg you to hide me
under your skirts.

DON CARLOS: Be quiet, you fool!

CASTAÑO: If one can find sanctuary
in the skirts of a priest,
why not in the skirts of a lady?[22]

DOÑA ANA (*aside*): It's Carlos, God help me!
Chance brings me
the opportunity
to honorably win his love
without risking
my precious reputation.
A show of nobility
in offering him sanctuary here
will disguise my love
under the cloak of compassion.
Without tarnishing
my good reputation,
I'll be able,
without surrendering to him,
to oblige him to surrender to me.
Although he loves Leonor,
when has being in love
ever given a man
enough will power
to resist a new temptation?
So lofty Love, do not hesitate,
for I know from my own experience
how easily you change.

(*aloud*) Señor,[23] misfortunes
give birth to courage
and lead to charity;
so, if your misfortune depends
on me to relieve them,
take time to catch your breath
in this room[24] which opens

onto the garden. Go in quickly,
before my brother arrives.
You'd have to prepare
for another duel if he
suspected you were alone with me.[25]

DON CARLOS: Señora, I wouldn't want
to cause you any harm
in granting me sanctuary.

CASTAÑO: Now you think of that?
God help me!

DOÑA ANA: Nothing frightens me.
Come, my brother
never comes in this room,
where we keep the ornate furniture
we use for
formal visitors
with carpets, chairs,
and other things. Besides,
it has an exit
into the garden if it's needed.
Don't worry about anything.
Come and I'll show you.
But first, to be careful,
I will lock the door,
so we'll be warned
of my brother's arrival by his knocking.

CASTAÑO *(aside to DON CARLOS)*
Señor, such a wealthy house!
And such a gallant lady!
I have a gut feeling
(and I certainly feel my gut
since it's empty),
that it's a shame you didn't
fall in love with this lady instead of Leonor,
whose wealth is only
in her brains?[26]

DON CARLOS: For God's sake, be quiet!

DOÑA ANA: Go in.
(*aside*)   Love, since you tempt me with this destiny,
                do not deny the rewards of this opportunity.

(*They exit.*)

SCENE TWO

[ON THE STREET][27]

(*DON RODRIGO and HERNANDO enter.*)

DON RODRIGO: What are you saying, Hernando?[28]

HERNANDO: What happened:
             that my mistress was taken from the house.

DON RODRIGO: But you do not know who could have done
              it?

HERNANDO: How could I, Señor Don Rodrigo, when,
             as you know, her beauty
             and intelligence were celebrated
             throughout Toledo and beyond?
             With all those suitors, I couldn't know
             which flirtation, which courtesy, was love.
             I suspect that you may be blamed,
             since you imprudently allowed so many men
             to pursue her oblivious to
             the obvious great danger.
             Greatly admired and pursued, she simply
             rewarded one of her suitors.

DON RODRIGO: Hernando, you test my patience;
              this is not the time for a warning.
              What a cunning beast! Who would have thought,
              with her display of honor and prudence,
              that such calculating hypocrisy,

such overwhelming lasciviousness, were hidden
in her treacherous heart?
Oh women! Such poisonous monsters![29]
Who could trust you
when, with equal insanity and audacity,
the stupid ones and the smart ones
are lost the same way.
I thought, vile daughter, that
in spite of my poverty,
your beauty, along with your intellect,
would be the greatest dowry I could offer.
Now, with what you have done,
that gain becomes your greatest loss.
The fact that you are well-known, famous,
and celebrated as a miraculous novelty,
only serves to make the story
of your disgrace better known.
But why do I wallow in laments
instead of seeking my revenge?
Why? Because I know the crime
I mourn, but not the criminal.
I am left dishonored, without knowing
how or against whom I can take my revenge.

HERNANDO: Señor, although I don't have any proof
of who took Leonor away,
rumor has it that
of the many suitors she had,
the most likely culprit
to have taken her is Don Pedro de Arellano.

DON RODRIGO: If it was Don Pedro,
could he not have allowed me
to deliver the woman[30] to him
without causing me such great dishonor?

HERNANDO: Señor, like all the suitors who
loved Leonor, desired her hand,
and begged you for it,
he feared that he would not be chosen.

All suitors are fearful
and none think they'll be favored.
Although I understand this fear,
I don't approve of such a remedy.
To prevent losing her, clearly
he sought to guarantee success by abducting her.
So, Señor, take my advice—
you're old and tired,
Don Pedro's young, rich, and brave,
and, after all, the damage has already been
    done—
act discreetly, as I suggest,
and offer him what he's taken.
Tell him to bring beautiful Leonor back home
and marry her at once.
He'll agree to it, for it would
restore his own honor.
By doing what I advise
you'll convert the poison into the cure.

DON RODRIGO: Oh Hernando! What treasure is more
    precious
than a faithful friend or loyal servant!
I have decided to find the culprit quickly
and convert my enemy into my son-in-law.

HERNANDO: Applying the remedy is always best,
Señor, before the disease is manifest.

(*They exit.*)

SCENE THREE

[IN THE HOUSE, LATER THAT NIGHT,
THE ROOM IS TOTALLY DARK.]

(*DOÑA LEONOR enters, fleeing from DON JUAN.*)

DON JUAN: Wait, fatal beauty!

Why do you run? Who offends you?
How will you respond to one who hates you,
if this is how you treat one who loves you?
You offend the very conquest
you sought to win,
since after conquering me,
you turned away from me.
In doing so, you created
two opposing actions:
you flee from one who loves you;
I follow one who kills me.[31]

DOÑA LEONOR: Señor, or whoever you are,
since I just arrived
in this house,
whose owner I don't even know,
how could you think that
I could listen to your words
which only frighten me
when I hear them?
If, as I suspect,
you think I'm someone else,
disabuse your passion.
Stop and think. Look at me
more carefully. I'm not
the woman you seek.

DON JUAN: Ungrateful woman!
You pretend the only reason
for not listening to my longings
is that my love has
so little honor in it.
Past experiences
should be enough
to assure you of my love.
It often seems that when
the most anxious
waves of passion come,
wanting to drown the shore
with the desires of love,

                your honor restrains
                the sea of my hopes.

DOÑA LEONOR: I already told you, I'm not
                who you think I am. Enough!
                Go away or I'll call
                for someone to hear these longings
                and reward them as truth
                or punish them as lies.

DON JUAN: Listen to me.

DOÑA LEONOR: I refuse.

DON JUAN: I swear to God, you tyrant,[32]
                that I'll force you to hear me,
                if you won't do it voluntarily.
                One must speak rudely
                to one bored with courtesy.

(*He grabs her arm.*)

DOÑA LEONOR: What is this? God help me!

DON JUAN: You call for God in vain.
                The one who calls for pity
                is always the one who lacks it.

DOÑA LEONOR: My God! Is there no one
                to protect my honor?

(*DON CARLOS enters, followed by DOÑA ANA.*)

DOÑA ANA: Stop. Wait.
                I'll see what it is,
                without you endangering yourself,
                in case it's my brother arriving.

DON CARLOS: Señora, that voice pierced my soul
                like a sword. Forgive me!

Trials: Act One

DOÑA ANA (*aside*): I locked the door,
so I'm sure it's not
my brother. I am more
concerned that Carlos
doesn't find his lady.
But if she was in my room
and Celia was with her,
what could this noise be?
It's so dark in here.
(*aloud*) Who's there?

DON CARLOS: It's me, Señora.
Why do you ask?

DON JUAN: Doña Ana, my love,
why do you treat me so cruelly?
What of the promises,
what of the words
you said to me in Madrid
which raised my hopes?
Obedient to your will,
like a moth to your flame,[33]
a sunflower to your beams,
a Clytie[34] to your clear light,
I left the comfort of my home,
the respect of my father,
and the affection of my homeland
to serve you.
Although it may have been
more courtesy than love,
your silent approval
was enough to make me
believe it was love.
I thought my hope was received
as an offering, a sacred
sacrifice, at your altar.
How could you treat me
so scornfully, so cruelly, now?

DOÑA ANA (*aside*): God, what do I hear?
Isn't that Don Juan de Vargas

        condemning my ingratitude
        and praising his loyalty?
        Who let him in here?

DON CARLOS: Señora, listen.

(*DON CARLOS grabs DOÑA LEONOR.*)

DOÑA LEONOR: Let me go, Señor.
        I already told you to leave me alone.

DON CARLOS: Listen to me, beautiful Doña Ana,
        I am Don Carlos, the one
        you offered sanctuary.

DOÑA LEONOR (*aside*):   My God! I thought he said, "Don
        Carlos!"
        I could have sworn
        it was Don Carlos' voice.
        As I have Carlos in my soul,
        so everyone sounds like Carlos to me,
        although I know my beloved
        is in prison.

DON CARLOS: Señora?

DOÑA LEONOR: Go away!
        I told you to leave me alone!

DON CARLOS: If you are angry
        because I followed you,
        forgive me. I only came
        to defend you
        if someone threatened to harm you.

DOÑA LEONOR (*aside*):   God help me! He sounds like Don
        Carlos.

DON JUAN: So, you ungrateful woman,
        you scorn me, do you?

(*CELIA enters with a light.*)

CELIA (*aside*): I came to see if my mistress is here,
so that Don Juan, who I left hiding
in her room could sneak out.
But what do I see?

DOÑA LEONOR (*aside*): What is this? Heaven defend me!
Isn't this Carlos I see?

DON CARLOS (*aside*): Unless I'm deceived,
this is Leonor!

DOÑA ANA (*aside*): Don Juan here?
I'm speechless!

DON JUAN (*aside*): Why is Don Carlos here?
He must be Doña Ana's lover.
Because of him that
treacherous and unfaithful woman
treats me with scorn.

DOÑA LEONOR (*aside*): My God! Is Carlos in this house,
while I lovingly wept
for him being in prison?
In a darkened room
does he make love to me
thinking it's someone else?
He must be this lady's lover.
But how can that be?
Is all this an illusion?
They brought me to him as a prisoner
and left me here! I'm
drowning in a sea of sorrows.

DON JUAN: You're no better than a whore![35]
You scorn me, but
you keep a man hidden
in your house? My God!
For this you scorned me?

>   Because chivalry requires
>   respect for women,
>   my anger cannot
>   avenge your ill treatment of me.
>   Although I'll spare you my cruelty,
>   I swear to God, you traitor,
>   I'll take vengeance on your lover!

DOÑA ANA: Stop, Don Juan, take care!

DON CARLOS (*aside*): Such confusions
                rage in my heart,
                that I'm astounded
                by what I hear.
                Stunned by everything,
                I understand nothing.
                My God, how did Leonor get here?

DOÑA ANA: Stop!

DON JUAN: Let go, traitor;
                I'll kill your lover!

CELIA: Señora, your brother's at the door.[36]

DOÑA ANA: What did you say, Celia? My God!
              —Gentlemen, if you care at all
              about my reputation, you must hide
              so I won't appear guilty
              to whomever is at the door.
              I give you my word
              that tomorrow you'll discover
              the cause of all your doubts.
              If my brother finds you here,
              my life and honor are in danger.

DON CARLOS: Rest assured that I
                will obey you, because
                I owe you so much
                for saving my life.

Trials: Act One

DON JUAN: And I, ungrateful woman,
although you have offended me,
since you command it,
I obey, for you are more obliged
to me if I obey you.

DOÑA ANA: Thank you for your concern.
—Celia, hide these two men
in separate rooms. I don't think
either of you will be able
to leave until morning.

CELIA: It will be morning soon.
—Don Juan, come with me.
—Señora, you can take that vision
wherever you want.

(*CELIA and DON JUAN exit.*)

DOÑA ANA: Señor, hide in this room.

DON CARLOS: I obey you.
I wish to God
this confusion was over!

(*He exits.*)

DOÑA ANA: Leonor, could you withdraw
as well?

DOÑA LEONOR: Even if you didn't order it,
I'd hide my shame, Señora.

(*She exits.*)

DOÑA ANA: Who ever saw so many confusions
happen in the short space
of less than an hour?
I can hardly catch my breath!

(*CELIA enters.*)

CELIA: Señora, I hid Don Juan
in my room. What do you want now?

DOÑA ANA: Go down and let my brother in;
that's all that matters now.

CELIA (*aside*): She's so stunned
she forgot to ask
how Don Juan got in the house.
But the danger passed,
so I won't have to make up a lie,
and lay the blame
on one of the other maids.
It's true that where there are many
who betray confidences,
some are accused by others
and some are excused by others.

(*She exits.*)

DOÑA ANA: God, what trials I've endured:
in love with Carlos,
pursued by Don Juan,
with my rival in my house,
with maids who betray me,
and my brother watching me!
But he's here; I'll dissemble.

(*DON PEDRO enters.*)

DON PEDRO: Señora, dearest sister,
How well you show your love
and how well you repay my affection!
The Sun found you awake,
and Dawn saw you dressed.[37]
Where did you put Leonor?

DOÑA ANA: In my room. I told her to

go to bed, brother, just
as you arrived.
But why are you so late?

DON PEDRO: Because on leaving her house
Leonor was recognized by her cousin,
whom Don Carlos nearly killed
with a thrust of his sword.
I saw him on the street
at dawn, although my servants
didn't know who he was or who did it.
So that this disturbance
wouldn't call attention to my plan,
I gave orders to my servants,
as if moved by pity,
that two of them tend to his wound
and take him to his house.
Meanwhile, the others seized Leonor
and Carlos, taking them
in order to deliver her to you.
Until the street was quiet,
I didn't dare to come home.

DOÑA ANA: It was a wise precaution.
You avoid many risks
with just this one delay.

DON PEDRO: You are discreet in everything.
If it seems to you
that Leonor is resting quietly,
I won't disturb her.
Since she's in my house,
there'll be plenty of time
for her to hear my suit.
No lover sees to
his own comforts before
those of his lady.
You may also go to bed,
for you have already
lost too much sleep

     trying to aid my desires.

DOÑA ANA: Brother, I would run greater risks
     to serve you.
     We two are as one;
     my soul treats
     your pains as its own,
     so that in considering your concerns
     I believe that your anxieties and mine
     stem from the same cause.

DON PEDRO: I thank you for your kindness.

DOÑA ANA (*aside*): If you understood my words . . .

DON PEDRO: Let's try to rest,
     if one who is in love can rest.

DOÑA ANA (*aside*): I'll rest a little,
     if one can rest who is in love.

DON PEDRO: Inspired by Love, my hope does all it can.

DOÑA ANA: Deceitful Love, assist my devious plan.[38]

(*They exit.*)

Notes for Act I

1. The literal English translation of *Los empeños de una casa*, *The Trials of a House*, is awkward in English and implies that the house undergoes trials rather than Leonor and Carlos. Scholars believe that Sor Juana's title intentionally parallels Calderón's title *Los empeños de acaso* [*The Trials of Chance*]. Variant translations of Sor Juana's title in English language criticism include *The Obligations of a House* (Wilkins), *The Desires of One House* (Williamsen), and *The Trials of a Noble House* (Flynn and Merrim).

2. *Castaño* literally means chestnut, so the name could be Anglicized and the character called "Chestnut."

3. In the premiere production, the sword fight described by Leonor was enacted while she narrated, so the character of Carlos' opponent, Diego, was added to the cast.

4. The character of Hernando was played by a woman in this production, so a feminine form of the masculine name Hernando was used.

5. The opening scene is written in *redondillas*, stanzas of four lines in an A-B-B-A rhyme scheme.

6. Literally, Ana says she was "left all alone," meaning without the male protection considered necessary to defend a woman's honor in the Spanish Golden Age.

7. In the original Spanish text, Ana speaks vaguely of the baseness of love, because Golden Age propriety would not have allowed her to speak more specifically.

8. Sor Juana uses the term, *señora*, as a title of respect for aristocratic women, whether or not they are married.

9. Literally, she asks, "Because he is already so much mine, what have I to long for?"

10. In Golden Age poetry, the Greek god, Apollo, represents ideal masculine beauty.

11. Literally, Celia says that Juan wants "to do the Tarquin." Sextus Tarquin, son of the tyrant Tarquin the Proud, raped the virtuous Lucretia in ancient Rome. Sor Juana uses the allusion to tactfully indicate Juan's crude intentions.

12 With the entrance of the masked men, the verse form changes to *romances*, stanzas of four lines with the second and fourth lines ending in assonant rhymes. Celsa Carmen García Valdés notes that 81.6% of the lines in *The House of Trials* are in the *romance* form, the most common verse form in Golden Age drama, often used both for action and narration.

13 The word *relación* could also mean "goings on" or "much ado," but the play contains many self-reflective lines, so such theatrical allusions are emphasized in this translation.

14 The formal, overly courteous humility of this paragraph, which is one very long sentence in the original, is difficult to render in English. Since Sor Juana herself was known for her amazing intellect, this part of the speech may be an ironic self-reference. In the premiere production of this translation, this section of the speech (from "They may interest you . . ." to ". . . the principle cause of my downfall.") was cut by the translator, who also directed the production.

15 In this paragraph and the next, Sor Juana seems to be describing her own life at court, and many critics assume that this section of the speech is autobiographical.

16 Although Leonor mentions Carlos' name in the previous sentence, Ana does not react to this piece of information until several minutes of performance time have passed. In the premiere production of this translation, Ana's aside that immediately follows Leonor's long speech was inserted here. (The part of Ana's speech addressed to Leonor remained where it was in the Spanish text.) This change allowed the actress playing Ana to react more naturally to the discovery that Leonor loves the same man she loves, and it added variety to this usually long exposition speech.

17 Literally, "the everlasting bond of Hymen," the Greek god of marriage.

18 The speaker, later identified as Don Diego, addresses someone named Don Juan in the Spanish text. This probably is not the same Don Juan from Madrid who loves Ana, since he is in her house. Juan is a common Spanish name, so it could easily refer to someone else.

19 In the original, these fourteen lines form a rhymed sonnet, a common form for soliloquies in Golden Age drama. The versification returns to the *romance* form with the entrance of Carlos.

20 The word in Spanish, *galán*, means the leading man in a play, as well as a suitor, courtier, or handsome man.

21 Literally, Carlos calls his escape "a noble cowardice," because it was ignoble for an aristocrat to flee from an aristocratic enemy, but acceptable for a nobleman to flee from the police.

22 Literally, Castaño says he seeks sanctuary in the *sacristán*, which means both a sacristan and a hoop-skirt or farthingale.

23 Literally, she addresses him as *caballero*, meaning gentleman.

24 She uses the word *cuadra*, meaning a spacious room.

25 According to the Spanish honor code, a woman's honor could be ruined if she was discovered alone in a room with a man who was not her husband. The presence of Castaño does not protect her, because he is Carlos' servant, not her own.

26 Castaño refers to Leonor as having *bachillerías*, a feminine form of the word for a bachelor's degree. The term was used in the seventeenth century as a pejorative way to describe women with intellect or learning.

27 The original text gives no stage directions to indicate locations. Although this scene could take place in Rodrigo's house, the street would be a better setting, so that the only house depicted on stage is the house referred to in the title of the play.

28 The verse form for this scene switches from the *romance* form to *pareados*, rhymed couplets in lines of irregular length. The verse form changes from assonant rhymes to true rhymes and more formal diction whenever Rodrigo enters.

29 Sor Juana satirized this kind of unjust attack on women in her well-known poem *Sátira filosófica* (Philosophical Satire). For an English translation by Muriel Kittel, see *The Defiant Muse: Hispanic Feminist Poems from the Middle Ages to the Present*, Angel Flores and Kate Flores, eds. (New York: The Feminist Press, 1986), 21-23.

30 Note that Rodrigo refers to Leonor as "the woman" instead of as "my daughter."

31 In Golden Age drama, men often claim that unrequited love will kill them. They project this action onto the object of their desire, accusing the women of killing them (hence, Juan addresses her as "fatal beauty").

32 Juan's speeches are filled with epithets, such as *ingrata* (ungrateful woman), *tirana* (female tyrant), and *traidora* (traitress).

33 Literally, "a salamander to your rays."

34 Clytie was a nymph who loved Apollo, the sun god, and followed him as he journeyed across the sky. She was turned into a sunflower, which always follows the sun.

35 In the original text, he calls her *¡Fácil, liviana!*, which literally translates as "Woman of easy virtue, loose woman!"

36 Perhaps the sound of knocking signals Celia that Pedro is at the door.

37 These lines are in past tense, suggesting that the sun rose just before Pedro entered.

38 In the original, the last four lines exchanged between Pedro and Ana are symmetrically constructed with Ana imitating Pedro's diction as precisely as possible. To suggest this, the last two lines rhyme in iambic pentameter to form an English equivalent to Sor Juana's rhymed quatrain.

ACT TWO

[IN THE HOUSE, LATER THAT DAY]

(*DON CARLOS and CASTAÑO enter.*)

DON CARLOS: Castaño, I'm beside myself.

CASTAÑO: And I, who follow you everywhere,
was only by myself,
when I took a little nap.

DON CARLOS: Do you know what happened to me?
I thought it was a dream.

CASTAÑO: I know all about dreaming;
I also had a dream.
And I slept like a lady,
since the clothes, Señor,
that Leonor gave me as she left
served as my bed.

DON CARLOS: Did Leonor give you her finest
dresses[1] to carry last night?

CASTAÑO: Yes, Señor. Since I saved them,
it's only fair that they save me.

DON CARLOS: Where are they?

CASTAÑO: There. I used them as a mattress.
Since I carried them
they can carry me.

DON CARLOS: I saw Leonor in this house;
I'm losing my mind.

CASTAÑO: They say, Señor, that
whoever loses his cattle, listens for cowbells.[2]
Since you lost Leonor,

the frenzy has smashed you
into little pieces,
so you see little Leonors everywhere.
    But tell me what happened between you
and Doña Ana.
May God take pity on her,
as she took pity on me.
    When she began
to talk with you,
I decided to go to sleep,
because three's a crowd.

DON CARLOS: Castaño, that's malicious gossip.
What happened, as you know,
is that I broke in here,
fleeing from the police;
    and she graciously and politely
promised to protect me.
She brought me to this room
and told me that she was
    Don Pedro de Arellano's sister;
and that I should hide here,
so that when her brother arrived
he wouldn't encounter me.
    With such gallantry,
she promised this and that,
so that the greatest part
of her beauty was her courtesy.
    Praising me with wit and flattery,
she exaggerated so much that,
if I were vain,
I'd attribute it to love.
    But they are the vain whims
of youthful pride:
which mistakes courtesy
for licentiousness.
    And their mistaken malice,
satisfied with its own evil,
doesn't consider women honest
if they are polite.

And judged so unfairly
as not even worthy of scorn,
women never behave very well
when men treat them badly.
 The man whose vanity
takes offense at such courtesy
misinterprets the flattery
as unworthy of an honorable woman.³
 But, returning to what
happened to me,
she was extremely kind
to me, Castaño.
 I told her my story,
and she discreetly
agreed to arrange everything
for me to stay here,
 telling me not to worry,
that she was doing this
due to risks she would run
if I revealed my presence,
 which I never
would have done,
if what I am about to tell you
had not happened.
 While we were talking
we heard what sounded like
the cries of a woman
in the next room.
 Although Doña Ana wanted
to prevent me from going in,
I stubbornly succeeded in
entering the room by force.
 A maid brought a light
to the sound of the voices, and with that
I could recognize beautiful
Leonor.

CASTAÑO: Who?

DON CARLOS: My Leonor.

CASTAÑO: Leonor? Were you dreaming?
What foolishness is this?
I thought you were a little crazy,
but not certifiably mad.
   Hearing this scares me.
Señor, take it easy!
You see, it's very good to be a little loony,
but it's no good to be this crazy.
   Madness is useful if,
like the waning and waxing of the moon,
it comes and goes,
for it helps in being valiant.
   But not, Señor, so that
your madness makes the neighbors
spy on you
and call you a half-wit.

DON CARLOS: Fool! if we were
at home . . .

CASTAÑO: Wait, Señor;
I saw Leonor, too.

DON CARLOS: Where?

CASTAÑO: In your pocket,
painted in all her splendor.
I thought it was alive,
because as soon as I looked at it,
it seemed to blush.[4]
   Although I'm not sure
(since I'm not very smart),
I thought, seeing it change,
that she had used rouge.

DON CARLOS: What nonsense!

CASTAÑO: Are you offended
that it seemed alive to me?
I've seen some women

Trials: Act Two 75

who were both alive and painted.

DON CARLOS: Why would Leonor want to paint her face?
In beauty she is the Sun.[5]

CASTAÑO: If she's the Sun, what's that
shining outside?
But if you saw Leonor, tell me,
what are you resolved to do?

DON CARLOS: I want to wait until I see
what brought her here.
If my merciful star[6]
allowed her to come here,
how could I leave
and abandon her?
So, it's better to wait
until everything's resolved,
to see if Fortune will provide
a chance to take her with me.

CASTAÑO: Well said. But, Señor,
someone's heading this way.
It looks like the maid.

(*CELIA enters.*)

DON CARLOS: I wonder what she wants?

CELIA: Señor, my lady
asks you to go
into the garden immediately,
because her brother must come
in here now, and it's better
if he doesn't see you.
(*aside*) Actually, it's so that he won't
be here to see Leonor.

DON CARLOS: Tell her I responded
obediently.

(*He exits.*)

CELIA: I must return.

CASTAÑO: Do you hear, and will you listen to me?

CELIA: What should I hear?

CASTAÑO: My confession.

CELIA: The greatest liar uses
the sweetest words.

CASTAÑO: Then I say, isn't it a confession
to speak of my sins?

CELIA: Don't rush at my affections,
I'm not free.[7]

CASTAÑO: Since you've imprisoned us,
can't I get you at a bargain rate?

CELIA: I already told you not to love me.

CASTAÑO: What does your honor require,
if I can't escape
my imprisonment and your love?
But, being a servant, what gives you such airs?

CELIA: You call me a servant, you louse?

CASTAÑO: Shut up! I shower you with attention
so you'll be nice to me.[8]

CELIA: I must go. But later,
If it's not a game, I'll be back.

CASTAÑO: It is a game; but you know
it's now your turn.

(*CASTAÑO and CELIA exit.*)⁹

(*DOÑA LEONOR and DOÑA ANA enter.*)

DOÑA ANA: How did you sleep last night, Leonor?

DOÑA LEONOR: Please, Señora,
don't ask me to tell you.

DOÑA ANA: Why?
(*aside*) It's a painful duty
to be compelled to humor
this woman who irritates me!

DOÑA LEONOR: Because if you ask me,
I must tell whether
I slept well or badly.
In either case
I encounter an objection.
My sorrows and your favors
are so mismatched,
that if I said I slept badly,
it would be rude,
and if I said well, it would be a lie.

DOÑA ANA: Your intellect and your beauty
war against one another.
It's a pity one so wise
is also so beautiful.

DOÑA LEONOR: When you are so sure
that you surpass everyone
in beauty, you easily
show affection
by praising mine,
which does not rival yours.

DOÑA ANA: Leonor, how are you feeling?

DOÑA LEONOR: Like someone
shipwrecked amid the tempests
of a stormy sea,
with the keel aground
and the stern in the air.
(*aside*) How can I ask her—
because I'm afraid to know—
why Carlos was here last night?
But why do I fear
the sting of jealousy
when so many torments drown me?

DOÑA ANA: Leonor, why do you hesitate?

DOÑA LEONOR: Forgive me, but I'd like to know
what Carlos said to you.
It would be devious of me
to pretend not to care
about what you know,
especially since I need to know it.
And so, Señora, I ask you—
since you already know I love
Carlos and that we're engaged—
How did he get in here last night?

DOÑA ANA: Allow me to delay the answer
to your question until later.

DOÑA LEONOR: Why?

DOÑA ANA: Because I want you
to listen to a musical diversion.

DOÑA LEONOR: It would divert my anxieties
more to have an answer to what
concerns me.

DOÑA ANA: I answer by telling you
that it was only a coincidence.
But here comes my brother.

DOÑA LEONOR: Then it would be best
for me to hide.

DOÑA ANA: No, on the contrary;
I told him about you,
because he might be able
to relieve your anxieties.
In the end, men are best
at settling these affairs
of ours.

DOÑA LEONOR: You argue well,
but I don't think I believe it.
(*DON PEDRO enters.*)
But, my God! what do I see?
Is this your brother, Señora?

DON PEDRO: I am, lovely Leonor.
Does that surprise you?[10]

DOÑA LEONOR (*aside*): Alas!
I'm speechless! Fortune,
you decree my downfall
in bringing me to
Don Pedro's house!

DON PEDRO: Lovely Leonor,
you are safe in my house.
Although it may cost me
my life and my immortal soul,
I know how to protect your honor
from the risks that threaten it.

DOÑA LEONOR: I thank you for your noble
concern, Señor Don Pedro.

DON PEDRO: Señora, since the waves
of your misfortune
cast you on this shore,
there is no need to say that you need

someone to help you with them.
　　　　I am yours, Señora.
Although you have always
treated me scornfully,
the scorn only tests my honor,
whose most gracious desire is
being polite at all costs.
You are in my house, and so
we will treat you now
by pleasing you and serving you
as the master of the house.
—Sister, entertain Señora Doña Leonor.

DOÑA ANA: Celia!

(*CELIA enters.*)[11]

CELIA: What are your orders, Señora?

DOÑA ANA: Tell Clori and Laura to sing.
(*aside to CELIA*)　In order for me
to reap the benefits
of the ingenious deceit
I've arranged, take Don Carlos
behind that lattice, so that
he sees us, but Leonor
cannot see or hear him.[12]
In this way, I'll arrange
for a jealous passion
to begin to enter his heart.
Although jealousy can
ignite love,
its operation is very different
on a suitor than
on a man about to be married.
What inspires love for a lady
inspires rage against a bride.
—Aren't you going to tell them to sing?

CELIA: I'll take care of both things.

DON PEDRO: In spite of everything, lovely Leonor,
               give me permission to break
               the laws of my silence
               with my amorous complaints.
               A man in pain must
               publicly proclaim his sorrow.
                    What defect do you see in my love,
               that you treat me so
               scornfully? Is my polite
               adoration an offense?
               If loving you is a crime,
               why is another man rewarded?
               Although equally guilty, why do we
               not share the same punishment?
               If in your beauty
               disdain must be the law,
               why is the law enforced with me
               but repealed for another?
               How was it that with you
               his passion was more successful,
               his pain was better rewarded?
               Although we felt the same,
               why did you think it was sinful in me
               and saintly in another.
               If he seemed more deserving,
               could the excess of my love
               compensate for what
               I lack in gallantry?
               Undoubtedly, my good qualities
               are what keep me from the reward.
               The least deserving
               are always the most successful.
               But if I must adore you
               forever, what does it matter
               if you deny me the reward?
               It is enough to know
               that you realize my nobility
               in denying me your mercy.

DOÑA LEONOR: I concede, Señor Don Pedro,

that you do me much honor.
I beg you, by who you are,
to do me a greater honor;
since you see that misfortune
has already drowned me,
do not add to my suffering.
It is enough that I am pulled down
by the cord of my shame
and the weight of my griefs.
Making love to me
while you see me
in such a state
is so inappropriate
that you should not say it
and I must not hear it.
I beg you to be silent.
If this is the revenge your love
takes on my scorn,
chose another form;
because I have too much suffering already
without you adding more.

(*They talk aside while DON CARLOS, CASTAÑO, and CELIA appear behind the lattice screen.*)

CELIA: Although my mistress ordered
that you remain hidden
'til you can leave here,
I want to give you the pleasure
of hearing from this latticed room
an excellent musical entertainment
that my master arranged
for a certain lady he loves.
Wait here.

CASTAÑO: Listen to me.

CELIA: I can't now.

(*She exits and re-enters on the other side of the lattice.*)

CASTAÑO: She goes and locks the door,
and leaves us like nuns
behind a screen. All we need is
a mother superior standing over us.[13]
(*He looks through the grating.*)
But God damn it, Señor!
Your madness is contagious;
I've caught it.

DON CARLOS: What are the symptoms?

CASTAÑO: I hear the cowbells
and the horns of the cattle
that we lost.

(*DON CARLOS looks through the grating.*)

DON CARLOS: What do I see? Love help me!
It's Leonor, Doña Ana, and
Don Pedro! You see what I saw
was no illusion.

CASTAÑO: Doesn't this anger you?

DON CARLOS: Not until I know why she's here.
If I'm in this house honorably,
without betraying her,
what makes you think that I suspect
Leonor of betraying me? Instead,
I believe that merciful Fortune
brought her where I am.

CASTAÑO: You love very calmly,
since you aren't usually this sane.
But aren't we being too good,
since, given the opportunity,
a man like Don Pedro
would seize it by the tail?

DON CARLOS: Shut your mouth, Castaño!

A man who would listen to
unfounded insults against
his lady is despicable.
The more jealousy he feels
the more he dishonors her.
But listen; they are tuning.

DOÑA ANA: Begin the singing.

CELIA: Listen to those scales![14]

SINGER A:[15] What could be the worst of pains
In all the sorrows love contains?

SINGER B: Lacking favor is the worst,
Since it is most often cursed.

SINGER A: It is not so.

SINGER B: It must be so.

SINGER A: What is the answer, do you know?

SINGER B: Worst of all are sleepless nights,
Caused by jealous pangs and plights.

SINGER A: It is not so.

SINGER B: It must be so.

SINGER A: What is the answer, do you know?

SINGER B: The pain of the impatient one,
Longing for the absent Sun.

SINGER A: It is not so.

SINGER B: It must be so.

SINGER A: What is the answer, do you know?

SINGER B: Concern about your love's welfare
               When your love is in your care.

SINGER A: It is not so.

SINGER B: It must be so.

SINGER A: What is the answer, do you know?

SINGER B: When the love has been returned,
               Not to possess the love you've earned.

SINGER A: It must be so.

SINGER B: It must be so.

SINGER A: You at last have answered right
               And know the pains of love's delight.

BOTH SINGERS: What could be the worst of pains
                   In all the sorrows love contains?

DON PEDRO (*to Leonor*):
               Of all the reasons the singers gave, the worst
               For me would be the one they mentioned first;
               Since the severest pain of love ignited
               Is the pain of love that's not requited.
               It's worse than death, you know.[16]

DOÑA LEONOR: It is not so.

DON PEDRO: It must be so.

DOÑA ANA: I'm of another opinion, brother dear.
               It's jealousy that causes me to fear.
               Not only does one suffer a lover's absence
               One also suffers under envy's presence,
               Which strikes a mortal blow.

DOÑA LEONOR: It is not so.

DOÑA ANA: It must be so.

DOÑA LEONOR: Although I have not given it much thought,
    I know the greatest ill that Love has taught
    Is when the one who loves you in return
    Is gone, and so the need for him will burn
    And longing for him will grow.

DOÑA ANA: It is not so.

DOÑA LEONOR: It must be so.

DON CARLOS: Castaño, sleepless nights, it seems to me
    Are caused by fears of feeling jealousy.
    My fear of falling into a jealous fit
    Is worse than really suffering from it,
    which is excessive woe.

CASTAÑO: It is not so.

DON CARLOS: It must be so.

CASTAÑO: Señor, I say that Love insults us most
    By granting us a kitchen wench as host,
    When I have nothing valuable to show
    And give to her to prove I love her so,
    Because I lack the dough.

DON CARLOS: It is not so.

CASTAÑO: It must be so.

CELIA: The greatest irritation Love can bring
    Is suitors who don't give me anything.
    I wear old dresses and fast all day instead
    Of being smartly dressed and richly fed.
    Why must I patch and sew?[17]

DOÑA ANA: It is not so.

CELIA: It must be so.[18]

DOÑA ANA: Leonor, since the music did not
amuse you, let's go into the garden.
Perhaps it will relieve
your grief.

DOÑA LEONOR: What relief
could I have besides
the release of tears?

DON PEDRO: Let's go, scornful goddess.

DOÑA ANA (*aside*): Celia, you did as I ordered.
I'll give you one of my stylish dresses,[19]
if we reap the benefits of the deceit.

(*DON PEDRO, DOÑA ANA, and DOÑA LEONOR exit.*)

CELIA (*aside*): That's certainly giving[20] in style.
However, this "I'll give you"
when said by masters,
doesn't turn out to mean much,
since it always turns out
that if they order something
in order to give,
they give themselves the excuse
that they forgot to give the order
in order not to give.
But the plot thickens,[21]
I came to open the door.[22]
Don Juan,
who was my major concern,
was so careful,
that without me escorting him
he escaped quietly
by the garden door
with the key I gave him.
My mistress fell for the story
that one of the other maids
let him into her room—
thanks to my hypocrisy
and some false oaths

                    that I threw in
                    so freely
                    that she still trusts me.
                    Now, she has entrusted me
                    to continue the plot.
                    —Señor Don Carlos?

DON CARLOS: What is it, Celia? Alas!

CELIA: I came to see if you had
         heard the music.

DON CARLOS: Yes, and I thank you for your kindness.
             But tell me, Celia, why was that lady
             with Doña Ana and Don Pedro
             in this house?

CELIA (*aside*): The fish takes the bait. I'll reel him in.[23]
(*aloud*) That lady, Señor, ...
         but I can't tell you
         unless you first promise
         not to tell anyone.

DON CARLOS: I promise. Why is she here?

CELIA: I'm afraid, Señor, that it's a sin
        to gossip about other people;
        but since you insist on finding out
        and I insist on not telling,
        here it is, without
        me actually saying it:
        You know that this miracle
        of beauty is a lady
        my master adores.
            Last night, I don't know how
        or why, she went to his room.
        He courts her and entertains her,
        to what end I don't know.
        Nor can I in good conscience
        confirm that she is guilty.[24]

It could be that he wants her
to become a nun!²⁵
Forgive me, I can't
tell you what you asked.
It's better to hear
these things from other lips.

(*She exits.*)

DON CARLOS: Castaño, did you hear that?
This confirms my agony and death.

CASTAÑO: If she didn't actually say it,
how can I be sure of it?

DON CARLOS: Dear God, what do I hear?
Is it an illusion, a magic spell,
that has affected me?
Who am I? Where am I?
Am I not the one who
idolized her beauty,
courted her so courteously,
served her so discreetly,
that in reward for my honesty
I attained Leonor's favor?
At last I succeeded
in winning her hand in marriage,
making me the luckiest man
out of so many unlucky men.
Didn't she elope with me last night,
leaving her house and her father,
granting me the happiness
which so many sought?
Didn't the police take her away?
Then, alas!, how could I find her
so contented in the house
of Don Pedro de Arellano,
who courts her so lovingly?
And I . . . but why am I
not seeking vengeance

instead of merely talking about it?
But, my God, couldn't Leonor
have come to this house
by chance, without being
responsible for what happened?
And couldn't Don Pedro,
taking advantage of having
the miracle of perfection in his power,
have dared to play the valiant suitor,
reaping the benefits of the lucky chance
Fortune granted him,
without Leonor agreeing to
his bold intentions?
It could be what it seems;
but do I do my duty by allowing it?
Why do I suffer my rival to
entertain my lady,
to take advantage of
having her at his side
to court and woo her?
How could I be so faint-hearted
as to see it and know it
and do nothing to remedy it?
I swear to God, it's not so!
Come, Castaño, follow me.
We'll search for Leonor
in spite of all those
who'd keep her from me.

CASTAÑO: Señor, are you so reckless?
Don't you know there's
a legion of lackeys in this house?
Before you know it
they'll beat us
and treat us rudely,
if they're good servants.

DON CARLOS: Coward! What are you saying?
Although the skies may hurl thunderbolts,
the heavens vent their rage,

and hell unleash its terrors,
I must find her.

CASTAÑO: If it must be, let's go and do it now.
The next step from here
will be the gallows.

(DON RODRIGO and DON JUAN enter.)[26]

DON RODRIGO: Don Juan, since you are his friend,[27]
you must bring him to reason;
that is why I brought you with me
on this occasion.
You were the witness
to the insult he gave me
when he stole Leonor from me.
You could, with greater ease,
speak in this case
more impartially than I could.
 I have told you everything,
and in such a serious case
a third person always fares better
than the injured party.
When a man who is noble and honorably born,
represents himself,
however much he feels the affront,
the shame of having to seek a remedy
hampers the means
to cure his injury.

DON JUAN: Señor Don Rodrigo,
by the code of chivalry,
I promise to bring Don Pedro
to your way of thinking,
which I think he will agree with.
Also, I will not claim
credit to my skill
what belongs to your merit.
So that he cannot deny what happened,
let us, without warning him,

	go into the . . .
(aside)	But what do I see?
	Don Carlos de Olmedo,
	with whom I dueled last night?
	Ungrateful Doña Ana! Cruel Medusa![28]

(*CELIA enters.*)

CELIA (*aside*): Jesus Christ!
　　　　　　Don Juan and an old man
　　　　　　have already seen you, Señor.

DON CARLOS: It doesn't matter; nothing frightens me.

DON RODRIGO (*aside to DON JUAN*): Don Carlos is here.
　　　　　That will be a great obstacle
　　　　　considering what we came to do.

CASTAÑO: Señor, say your prayers.
　　　　　I think they've come
　　　　　to make dog meat of us.
　　　　　Clearly they already know
　　　　　you killed Don Diego
　　　　　and eloped with Leonor.

DON CARLOS: It doesn't matter; whatever happens,
　　　　　　I am determined to find her.

DON RODRIGO: It is better to face the issue;
　　　　　　I will approach him.
　　　　　　—Don Carlos: Don Juan and I
　　　　　　have come about a certain affair
　　　　　　which just now
　　　　　　must be discussed with Don Pedro.
　　　　　　So, if it is not a hindrance
　　　　　　to your business, I beg you to leave us
　　　　　　alone. Pardon
　　　　　　the inconvenience, that the old
　　　　　　take this license with the young
　　　　　　who are as generous and polite
　　　　　　as you are.

Trials: Act Two

DON CARLOS (*aside*): Dear God!
    Don Rodrigo doesn't know
    I'm the cause of his grievance.

DON JUAN (*aside*):   Dear God!
    I don't know how to restrain the rage
    Don Carlos incites in me.

CELIA (*aside to DON CARLOS*):   Don Carlos, you know
    the trials my mistress would suffer
    if her brother should see you.
    I beg you to keep out of sight.

DON CARLOS (*aside*): She is right, by God!
    If I'm seen by her brother
    I endanger Doña Ana's life.[29]
    Since she saved my life,
    it is wrong to put hers at risk.
    But what can I do in this case?
    There's no other remedy;
    I'll hide, since Doña Ana's
    honor is the primary concern.
    I'll go forth later to avenge
    my grievances and jealousies.

CELIA (*aside to DON CARLOS*):   Señor, for God's sake,
    hide before Don Pedro comes!

DON CARLOS: Señor Don Rodrigo,
    forgive me if I
    offend you, for your dignified
    gray hair deserves respect,
    but I'm in Don Pedro's house
    without his knowledge. So I beg you
    to allow me to hide
    before he comes. I'm obliged
    to avoid endangering someone's honor.

DON JUAN (*aside*):   How can I allow this!
    I must admit, what could be more obvious?
    Doña Ana, that evil Medusa,[30]

>   brought him here.
>   It kills me that
>   I haven't killed him!
>   But first the trials of
>   Don Rodrigo must be resolved,
>   since I promised to help him.
>   Afterwards, I'll come back,
>   since I have the key to
>   the garden, and take
>   the vengeance I desire.

DON RODRIGO: Don Carlos, nothing surprises me.
              Although I am old, I was young once
              as you are now. One must
              allow each season its fruits.
              I assume if you say
              it is necessary to remain hidden,
              that you are doing what is proper.
              I do not ask about the cause
              of affairs that do not concern me.

DON CARLOS: Then, I take my leave.

DON RODRIGO: God be with you!

CELIA: Hurry!
(*aside*)   Thank God
              he got himself out of this difficulty!
              —And you, Señor, wait while
              I tell my master that you're here.

DON CARLOS (*aside*): My soul burns like Mount Etna![31]

DON JUAN (*aside*):   My heart bursts like a volcano!

(*DON CARLOS, CASTAÑO, and CELIA exit.*)

DON RODRIGO: So goes the world:
              Don Pedro offends me,
              Don Carlos offends him,
              and then there will be

             a third to offend Don Carlos.
             This is how Heaven permits
             punishment for sins:
             arranging the crimes we receive
             as retribution for
             the crimes we commit.

DON JUAN (*aside*):   I'm so enraged
             at having to see the cause
             of my grievance that I don't know if
             I'll be calm enough
             to speak in the affair
             I promised to negotiate.
             Whoever ignores his own cause
             will speak badly in another's.

(*DON CARLOS and CASTAÑO appear behind the grating.*)

DON CARLOS (*aside*): I had to hide myself
             out of respect for Doña Ana, to whom
             I owe my sanctuary and my life,
             but I want to listen. From here
             I can see without being seen.
             When Don Rodrigo arrived,
             a thousand fears seized my heart.
             The astrology of my misfortunes
             warns of such disasters.

(*DON PEDRO enters.*)

DON PEDRO: Señor Don Rodrigo, you[32] come
             to my house? I am greatly indebted
             to the occasion that brings you here,
             since it kindly permits
             you to do me such honor.

DON RODRIGO: Señor Don Pedro, I am
             indeed honored by you,
             since I come to your house
             for the honor I have lost.

DON PEDRO: Señor Don Juan, my friend,[33]
it is not new that you honor my house.
—Please sit down and
tell me why you have come.

DON JUAN: I am at your service.
Since we come on a matter
that cannot be delayed, I will begin:
Señor Don Pedro, you well know
as an honorable gentleman
the many obligations
that you must undertake.
Despite that, Señor Don Rodrigo
has a disagreement with you.

DON PEDRO: With me, Señor Don Juan?
Please tell me what it could be.
(*aside*) God defend me! What is it?

DON RODRIGO: Señor Don Pedro,
There is no time
for pretense.
If you pretend not to know
our business out of respect
for my position,
I thank you for the courtesy,
but absolve you of the obligation.
You courted Leonor
as a passionate suitor
and could have asked me for her hand in marriage,
but by vile means
you stole her from my house,
an act which . . .[34] But I do not wish
to scold you now for the crime
for which I have no remedy.
It is better to be merciful,
since I seek mercy from you.
The more you make amends,
the less I need to forgive.

> Having said that, you already know
> there is no family in Toledo
> whose blood is nobler than mine.
> Since that is certainly true,
> what objection could you
> find in becoming my son-in-law?
> If you object because of my poverty
> and your wealth, that
> would have been a valid point
> if I had negotiated
> Leonor's marriage with you.
> But since you chose her
> without my consent,
> and put yourself in a position
> where you must marry her,
> I am absolved of the consequences
> of your rash behavior.
> You know that I could not
> suffer her presence in your house
> without you marrying her
> immediately.

DON PEDRO (*aside*): God defend me!
> What can I say to Don Rodrigo
> under such terrible trials?
> If I deny I have her,
> it's easy for him to discover the lie;
> and if I confess the truth
> that Don Carlos stole her,
> he'll give her to him and I'll lose her.
> If I lose Leonor, I lose my life.
> If he forced her to marry me,
> Leonor would despise me.
> Who could find a way
> to delay his command?

DON JUAN: Why do you hesitate, my friend,
> when his proposition
> secures your honor;
> when Señor Don Rodrigo,

so restrained and so discreet,
offers you the happiness
of being the fortunate owner
of Leonor's beauty?

DON PEDRO: First of all, I declare,
Señor Don Rodrigo,
that I worship the
beauty of Leonor.
Since you know I courted her,
you must know that
my heart could neither
see her with other eyes
nor speak to her with any other intent,
except that of being happy to have her
as my wife. But having said that,
you must know that Leonor heard last night
(for I cannot tell a lie)
that my sister, whom she regards
with tender affection, was ill;
and she came to my house
only to see her, believing
that you would be
playing cards until very late.
Time passed, and she grew afraid,
since she had left without permission,
that you had already returned.
So we sent a servant of mine
to find out,
and he returned to say
that you were at home
and noticed Leonor
was missing. Outraged,
you took the extreme but justifiable
action of searching for her.
She trembled when she heard this
and did not want to go home.
That is all that happened.
I did not steal Leonor;
nor could I, since

>   I hope to wed her beauty,
>   proceed so rudely that
>   I would tarnish the mirror
>   in which I hope to see my honor reflected.
>   And so that you don't assume
>   I invented this excuse
>   in order to avoid marriage,
>   I promise on my honor and my faith
>   to be her husband as soon as
>   Leonor agrees to it.
>   With this, you will understand
>   that I have no objection
>   to being your son-in-law
>   other than the fact that I don't deserve her.

DON CARLOS: Did you hear that, Castaño?
              I'm losing my life and my mind.

CASTAÑO: Losing your life is new;
           but losing your mind is old news.

DON RODRIGO: Señor Don Pedro, I do not wish
              to question what you have said.
              The events may or may not
              have happened as you stated.
              But seeing that your interest
              in Leonor is acknowledged by all,
              that Leonor was missing
              and I searched for her,
              and that I found her in your house,
              nothing would satisfy my honor
              but your marriage to her.
              It does not matter
              whether Leonor agrees or not
              to what you have proposed,
              since nothing could please her more
              than obeying my commands.
              So call her, and you will see
              how quickly the bargain is settled.

DON PEDRO: Señor, that may frighten Leonor.
So I beg you to wait until
my sister proposes it to her.
Although I believe that
I am ready to be married,
it has been arranged very suddenly.
What does it matter if we defer
this until tomorrow? That would allow time
for me to inform
my friends and relatives,
so they could attend the wedding.
And then we will bring
Leonor to your house
where the marriage will be performed.

DON RODRIGO: I agree. But swear
that we have settled this,
that Leonor is your wife.

DON PEDRO: You have my word on it.

DON RODRIGO: Then, my son, farewell. I also
wish to do my part
of the preparation.

DON PEDRO: Señor, let's go. I will escort you.

DON RODRIGO: That is not necessary. Stay here,
for you have much to do.

DON PEDRO: I must go with you.

DON RODRIGO: You must not.

DON PEDRO: Then I obey you.

DON JUAN: Señor Don Pedro, God be with you.

DON PEDRO: And with you, Señor Don Juan.

(*DON RODRIGO and DON JUAN exit.*)

DON PEDRO (*aside*): I'm so confused that I don't know
if I'm sad or happy,
fortunate or unfortunate,
in what happened to me.
Don Rodrigo insists that I marry
Leonor, and since I have her here,
the case is such that I can't
refuse to marry her.
Only I fear that
she will refuse me.
But recognizing the state of things
and the authority of her father,
perhaps she will
agree to be mine. I go.
May Love soften her heart!

(*He exits. DON CARLOS and CASTAÑO come out from behind the grating.*)

DON CARLOS: I must not be myself,
Castaño, if that didn't kill me.
Don Rodrigo, alas!, thinks
that Don Pedro took Leonor
and came to offer her to him.
And he, the smiling hypocrite,
arranges to marry her,
ignoring the fact
that she eloped with another.

CASTAÑO: What do you expect? That fellow's
eager to be a husband,
and he stops at nothing.
He sighted this flying heron
and wanted to shoot her down in flight.
Well then, since he bagged her,
your chances have flown the coop.

DON CARLOS: I'm so beside myself, Castaño;
I'm not sure I know what
to do about this.

CASTAÑO: I'll give you a good remedy
to serve as revenge.
Doña Ana is rich, and I think
she's bursting to be a bride.
Woo her, and with this
you're avenged by getting tons of money.
Do what will most
enrage this fool:
"in-law" him to death.

DON CARLOS: My God, what a fine revenge that would be!

CASTAÑO: Do you think it's bad advice?
You must not realize
that a father-in-law,
a step-mother, an old aunt,
a notary, an innkeeper,
a hired mule,
nor a lawyer,[35] whom I consider
the choicest inhabitants
in Hell, can't hold a candle
to a brother-in-law.

DON CARLOS: My God, what blasphemy![36] What could
I do in that case?
Oh, Leonor, if I lose you,
I lose my life as well!

CASTAÑO: Don't lose your head as well;
Let's look for her first.
As the Appeals Court
of her affections, she may
revoke his law.

DON CARLOS: What if her father forces her?

CASTAÑO: How can he force her? What's he
going to do, play the tyrant?[37]
Let's look for her now.
If she says no,

Don Pedro can't say yes.

DON CARLOS: Well said, Castaño; let's go.

CASTAÑO: Let's go and skip the cries of "alas!" and "alack!" that prevent our leaving and prolong the act.[38]

Notes for Act II

1 The Spanish word, *galas*, means finery or regalia, suggesting that Castaño has Leonor's fanciest court dresses.

2 In the original, Castaño only quotes the first phrase of this proverb, expecting Carlos and the audience to know the rest.

3 Sor Juana examines this unfair treatment of women at length in her poem *Philosophical Satire*, which is subtitled, "Arguing that there are inconsistencies between men's tastes and their censure when they accuse women of what they themselves cause." (*The Defiant Muse*, 21.)

4 Portraits and their ability (or inability) to capture the beauty of the sitter serve as the subjects for several poems written by Sor Juana. Some biographers believe that Sor Juana may have painted portraits herself.

5 The sun represents the epitome of perfect physical beauty in many Golden Age plays.

6 Despite the Catholic Church's stand against astrology, references to the influence of the stars appear in many Golden Age plays and throughout *The House of Trials*.

7 Celia's line has been altered to retain the financial pun in Castaño's next line, which is in the original.

8 Literally, "so you won't lose your manners."

9 Some editions indicate a change of scene here, but the dramatic action does not require it.

10 Pedro speaks to Leonor in the formal form (*vosotros*) rather than the familiar form (*tú*). She also uses this formal form when speaking to him, although she talks to Ana in the familiar form. Since modern English does not make this distinction, the translation suggests it through the use of extremely polite titles and very formal diction.

11 In the original, there is no stage direction here to indicate whether Celia has been on stage since her conversation with Castaño or if she enters now in response to Ana's command.

12 Literally, Ana says, "so that he sees us, but can hear nothing of our conversation." The change in translation clarifies the situation for the audience who needs to understand that Leonor cannot see or hear Carlos when he is hidden behind the grating or lattice.

13   In the original, Castaño says all they lack is an *escucha*, which was a nun who was present whenever another nun spoke to a visitor through the grating at a convent. The image refers to Sor Juana's own vocation.

14   Literally, Celia says, "She begins to sol-fa," to sing using the syllables "do, re, mi, fa, so, la, ti, do," or to sing the sol-fa scale.

15   In the original text, Music (as an allegorical character) appears as a singer in Ana's musical entertainment, which is a kind of quiz game. Music asks a question that five soloists attempt to answer, while two choruses determine the correct response. I have redistributed the lines between two singers—one asks the question and the other makes five attempts to answer it.

16   This speech and the five that follow it are written in a highly structured, eight-line verse form with an A-B-B-A, A-C-C-D rhyme scheme. All of the speeches end with the same rhyming word which also rhymes with the last line from the musical entertainment, "It is not so. It must be so." Reproducing this structure in English would wildly distort the content of the speeches and sound stilted. The speeches are translated into rhyming couplets of iambic pentameter, which sounds more natural in English, and a final line that rhymes with all the other final lines.

17   Literally, "I'm waiting for the relief of a dressmaker's thimble."

18   In performance, I suggest that music continue to play under the dialogue until this line. At this point, the musicians could have a final chorus and complete Ana's planned entertainment.

19   Literally, "I leave you a dress." In the seventeenth-century, aristocratic women often handed down their old dresses to their maids.

20   In the Spanish original, the verb is *mandar*, which means to order or to leave (as in a will). Celia's aside contains a series of untranslatable puns on the verb and the nouns based on that verb.

21   In the original, she uses the word *tramoya*, which literally means stage machinery, but is used in everyday speech to mean a trick or a deceit.

22   That is, to open the door for Carlos and Castaño, so they can come out from behind the grating.

23   Literally, "I loosen the sails" or "I set sail."

24   Literally, that she is *malo*, meaning evil or licentious.

25   Literally, "a discalced nun." Sor Juana first entered a convent of discalced (barefoot) nuns, but stayed there only three months. Later she joined a less rigid order. This sarcastic remark by Celia, being an autobiographical reference, would have been an "in-joke" for the original audience.

26 Apparently, Carlos and Castaño start to exit or move aside, so that Rodrigo and Juan do not see them. Some editors insert a scene change here, adding a stage direction indicating an exit for Carlos and Castaño and another indicating an entrance later.

27 As in Act One, the verse form changes when Rodrigo enters. His speech consists of two *décimas*, ten-line stanzas with true rhymes in A-B-B-A-A, C-C-D-D-C form. Juan begins his speech in this more formal style, but returns to the usual *romance* form when he sees Carlos.

28 Literally, he calls her a basilisk, a legendary reptile whose glance and breath were fatal. Medusa, a woman in Greek mythology who turned men into stone, offers an equivalent allusion which is more commonly recognized.

29 The mere presence of a man who was not a family member created an assumption of guilt and dishonor. The only remedies to restore the woman's honor were marriage to the man who dishonored her, life in a convent after the man was killed, or immediate death at the hand of her nearest male kin.

30 Again, he calls her a basilisk in the original.

31 Etna, even today, is a famous active volcano in Sicily.

32 Pedro and Rodrigo speak to each other in the formal, polite form of you (*vosotros*). The men mask their concerns with overly polite formalities.

33 Even though Pedro says they are friends, he uses the formal *vosotros* instead of the familiar *tú* when speaking with Juan.

34 Rodrigo loses his temper, but quickly masks his emotions with ritualized etiquette.

35 These common stereotypes were often ridiculed in seventeenth-century drama, especially crooked lawyers, greedy notaries, cheating innkeepers, and stubborn mules.

36 Literally, Carlos calls him "an infidel."

37 Literally, Castaño asks if the old man would be a Tarquin, the Roman tyrant who was overthrown after his son, also called Tarquin, raped Lucretia.

38 This is another self-reflective reference in which the characters acknowledge that they are in a play. Most of these references are spoken by either Celia or Castaño.

ACT THREE

SCENE ONE

[IN THE HOUSE, THAT NIGHT]

(CELIA and DOÑA LEONOR enter.)

DOÑA LEONOR: Celia, I'll have to kill myself,
if you won't allow me to leave
this house, or this enchantment.

CELIA: Control yourself, beautiful Leonor,
and think of your reputation.

DOÑA LEONOR: What would you have me think,
Celia, since I just heard
the horrible news,
that my father wants me,
dear God!, to be Don Pedro's wife,
because he mistakenly believes
that Don Pedro abducted me?
And on top of this
you yourself tell me
that my unfaithful lover, Carlos,
the one who could,
as my fiancé, free me
from the cruelty of this violence,
is in love with Doña Ana
and plans to marry her.
Being in this position,
my sorrows never cease;
with no refuge to relieve them,
nor advocate to aid them.

CELIA (*aside*): What she says is true,
and I have confused Don Carlos
with the same plot device,[1]
because my mistress ordered me
to enrage Doña Leonor,

　　　　　　　　　so she would love Don Pedro
　　　　　　　　　and no longer want Don Carlos.
　　　　　　　　　And I performed my part
　　　　　　　　　making up these lies
　　　　　　　　　in order to get the dress.
(*aloud*)　　　　　—If you know, Señora,
　　　　　　　　　that ungrateful Carlos abandoned you,
　　　　　　　　　and my master idolizes you,
　　　　　　　　　and your father wants
　　　　　　　　　you to marry Don Pedro;
　　　　　　　　　and that if you refuse to marry him
　　　　　　　　　under these circumstances,
　　　　　　　　　you lose your honor and a good match;
　　　　　　　　　isn't it better to agree to this
　　　　　　　　　and resolve it discreetly
　　　　　　　　　by going through with the marriage?
　　　　　　　　　It would be a pity to let this pass.
　　　　　　　　　And you'll find, if you do it,
　　　　　　　　　more than three thousand blessings;
　　　　　　　　　since with this one action you mend
　　　　　　　　　the loss of your reputation,
　　　　　　　　　you obey your father
　　　　　　　　　and please your family,
　　　　　　　　　and you reward the man who loves you
　　　　　　　　　and get revenge on Don Carlos.

DOÑA LEONOR:　What are you saying, Celia?
　　　　　　　　　Before I'd belong to Don Pedro,
　　　　　　　　　you'd see the stars fall
　　　　　　　　　from their eternal vault;
　　　　　　　　　the sea would break
　　　　　　　　　the passive reins
　　　　　　　　　that the bridle of sand
　　　　　　　　　imposes on the wild waves;
　　　　　　　　　the Sun, that fiery
　　　　　　　　　heart of the heavens,
　　　　　　　　　would cease to shine
　　　　　　　　　on the face of the Earth;
　　　　　　　　　reversing the order
　　　　　　　　　which Nature ordains,

Trials: Act Three   109

                     fire would freeze snowflakes,
                     and ice would emit sparks.
                     Before I'd stop loving Carlos,
                     although the ungrateful man rejected me,
                     I'd end my life
                     by killing myself.
                     Before I'd leave the one I love . . .

CELIA: Forget about the befores,
                     and get to the afters.
                     Since you're so determined,
                     I don't how to advise you
                     without knowing your plans.

DOÑA LEONOR: Since I entrusted my sorrows to you,
                     my friend, I want you
                     to give me a chance to escape
                     from here; so when my father
                     returns, he doesn't find me here
                     and marry me off by force.
                     I'll flee from here
                     to search for a convent cell,[2]
                     a hiding place to bury myself,
                     where I'll remain for the rest of my life,
                     weeping for my tragedy
                     and mourning for my sorrows.
                     Perhaps my fateful star won't
                     know I'm hiding there.

CELIA: Yes, but my star will find me.
                     If I let you leave,
                     my master would see stars
                     when he found out;
                     and then he'll make me see stars,
                     if you don't follow your star.

DOÑA LEONOR: Be a friend to me,
                     I beg you, and
                     I'll be yours forever,
                     although this is my first request of you.

CELIA: Even if it's the first,
if I did it
I'd pay too dearly for it.

DOÑA LEONOR: Then, damn you, you fiend!
If you won't let me leave,
I'll kill myself and kill you!

CELIA (*aside*): What fire and lightening!
Dear Jesus, what if
she attacks me now?
What can I do? If I don't let her
out and she becomes my mistress,
there'll be hell to pay.
And if I let her go,
I'll get the same
from my present master. So then,
it's best to put her off
and warn my master
what his lady's planning.
I know that he'll have to
stop her from leaving,
then I remain on good terms with both of them.
With this strategy,
she won't be offended by me
and he'll be grateful to me.
(*aloud*) —Señora, since you ordered this
and you're so determined
to do it, go get your veil
while I keep an eye on the door.

DOÑA LEONOR: Celia, you've given me life again.

CELIA: I've a soft spot in my heart,
and seeing tears makes me
melt like butter.

DOÑA LEONOR: I'm going to put on my veil.

CELIA: Go on, then; and come right back
while I wait.

(*DOÑA LEONOR exits.*)
>I won't do that,
>but I will lock the door instead
>and warn the Lord of Hades
>that his Persephone wants to escape.³

(*CELIA exits and DON JUAN enters.*)

DON JUAN: Using the key to the garden,
which Celia gave me
in order to obtain my happiness,
I come to investigate my suspicions.
How foolish to say "investigate,"
since the evidence
cannot be doubted!
I wish my jealousy and grief
were mere suspicions.
But when the offense is against my honor,
how can I risk
proving my dishonor
without preparing my defense?
If mere conjecture is enough
to offend me, how could my honor
presume doubt as
evidence of my grievance,
transforming that same evidence
of an offense against my honor
from a doubtful truth
to a true doubt?
Since suspicion alone
is enough to offend honor,
the man who assumes doubts are true
confirms his own dishonor.
Therefore, how could I imagine
that someone could offend me,
if I cannot prove beyond a doubt
that I have been offended?⁴
    Hidden here, I wait
for my enemy to come.
Considering the state of

his friendship with Doña Ana,
who doubts he'll come by night,
since he comes and goes by day.
I'll go inside and wait for him.
Honor, grant me the courage to defend you!⁵

(*DON JUAN exits and DON CARLOS enters with CASTAÑO carrying a bundle of clothes.*)

DON CARLOS: Although I went through the house,
I couldn't find her,
and I fall into despair.

CASTAÑO: But, Señor, didn't you notice
there were locked doors
which lead to that other room?
Are they locked for fear
of Doña Ana's brother seeing you
or of you finding Leonor?
In order to force you to marry her,
Doña Ana and her brother
have locked us inside.

DON CARLOS: Castaño, I've decided
Don Rodrigo should know
I was the man who eloped with his daughter,
who hopes to be her husband.
He intends to give her to Don Pedro,
because he thinks Don Pedro did it;
so he'd give her to me
if he learned the truth
about who abducted her.

CASTAÑO: You reason well,
but how will you get out
if Doña Ana is standing sentry
and keeping a close watch?

DON CARLOS: It would be easy, Castaño,
for me to escape against her will,

since I'm in no mood
to surrender
so easily.
But what stops me
and weakens my resolve
is leaving the house
while Leonor is still here.
I should be here in case
she needs my help.
So, I decided that you
should leave; even if they see you,
no one would take notice
of you as they would of me.
Take this letter in which
I've written the whole story
to Don Rodrigo.

CASTAÑO: By Saint Tecla![6]
How could you send me out there?
Don't you see that the police
could pick me up in the streets
as an accomplice in the
wounding of Don Diego?
Although you did it,
wouldn't I suffer for
aiding and abetting a crime?

DON CARLOS: It is my will, Castaño.

CASTAÑO: But it's not mine.

DON CARLOS: I swear on my life, you must go!

CASTAÑO: But Señor, what's the point
of swearing on your life
that I must lose mine?

DON CARLOS: Are you making a joke, Castaño?

CASTAÑO: No, I'm speaking the truth, Señor.

DON CARLOS: What is this, you traitor? Are you
trying to exhaust my patience?
You'll go, damn you,
or I'll kill you!

CASTAÑO: Hold it, Señor!
Since this death is imminent
and the other is contingent,
give me the letter and I'm gone.

DON CARLOS: Take it, and see that you return
quickly. I'll be waiting
impatiently.

CASTAÑO: Let me tell you a story, Señor,
that seems to the point here
(very much to the point).
 A man went to fight a bull
and begged for a horse from another man,
who couldn't refuse him
even though he wanted to.
 The owner couldn't stand,
seeing the horse go,
and sent the bullfighter a message telling
him to take good care of the horse
 because it was valuable.
The bullfighter very calmly replied,
"Don't tell me, tell the bull!"
 This is your position now:
You send me out on the street
where, although I want to,
I don't know if I'll make it back.
 And what makes me laugh
in such a painful situation
is that, although it's dangerous,
you tell me to come back quickly.
 So now I say to you,
like that bullfighter,
don't tell me,
tell Don Rodrigo!

(*CELIA enters.*)

CELIA: Señor Don Carlos, my mistress
asks you to see her
in the garden immediately.
She has something important
to discuss with you.

DON CARLOS: Tell her I obey her command.
(*to* CASTAÑO) And you obey my command.

(*DON CARLOS and CELIA exit.*)

CASTAÑO: I don't really want to do it,
since it would be better for me
to keep hidden.
 God help me! How could
I contrive to give Don Rodrigo
this letter without him
or anyone else recognizing me?
I wish Garatuza[7] was here!
In Mexico he's said to have
performed many miracles
while disguised as a priest.
Since I was born there,[8]
I always worshiped him
as the patron saint of my homeland.
 Oh, Garatuza, whoever you were,
whoever you are,
whether waving a fan
or wearing a sword;[9]
help me to escape these trials
by inspiring a scheme for me
worthy of the great playwright, Calderón![10]
 But wait! An idea for a
plot just struck me.
Leonor gave me some clothes
and jewelry to carry,
when she, like Helen of Troy,
ran off with Paris, her playmate.
I have them with me
'cause I used them for a bed.
If I dressed up in them,
what veiled lady in Toledo

could match my elegance?
Well then, I'll take these off;
throw these rags away!

(*He removes his hat, cloak, and sword.*)

First of all, I'll have to
tie up my long hair,
because a thousand lives will be lost
if I untie just a tiny bit.
With this cloth I'll try
to cover my head;
if I could put it on the way I want,
the glory would be worth the pain.
Now we get to the outer skirts.
Jesus, what gorgeous fabric!
It sure suits me,
since I'm a brunette[11]
and look as good as the sky in blue.
And what's this? Jewels!
I don't want to put them on now,
since I'm not fully dressed yet.
I found a kerchief
in this sack
that I simply must try on.
Does it cover the chest?[12]
I don't have any make-up.
Please God, let there be some.
I could really use
a make-up brush;
but no, that's unnecessary,
since I'll blush anyway.
I don't need any rouge,
for in this trial, of course,
I'll blush soon enough
like a bashful girl.
—Ladies,[13] how do you think
this whalebone corset fits?
Is it better with or without
the petticoats?[14]

I'm certainly beautiful.
Thank God, I'm pretty!
Anything looks good on me,
because I have a good figure.
I want to wear the accessories,
since I'm not a perfect lady without them.
The gloves, of course,
because the hands must not be seen.
They're as hairy as Jacob's
when he disguised himself with goatskins.[15]
The veil tops it off,
as I throw it over the top of my head.
Dear God, how much
this thin silken fabric covers!
No trapdoor[16] is so well-hidden,
no rampart so well-defended,
no robber so well-disguised,
no page lies so much,
no gypsy deceives so much,
no usurer gains so much.
The fan reflects
my own grace and beauty;
but if it blows hot air,
how could it be like me?
    A lady in the audience
says to her friend:
Margaret, this fool
is playing *El Tapado*.[17]
Please remember, ladies,
that this is a play.
Don't think that I
hatched this scheme myself.
I don't want to fool any of you,
especially not Your Excellency.[18]
    I am armed. And I wouldn't be surprised
if in the end four thousand suitors
will see me and follow me,
leaving behind the girls
they were courting
and flocking to fall in love with me,

                    without a thought for
                    the beauty of the others.
                    Come then, modesty,
                    mincing steps, haughty carriage,
                    and graceful manner.
                    Tilt the head
                    a little to the side.
                    Wrap the hand in the veil;
                    Hide one eye with it,
                    and reveal the other.
                    Let's go, since it's a waste
                    to lock up such beauty.
                    I'm afraid someone
                    will fall in love with me.

(*He starts to leave and meets DON PEDRO.*)

DON PEDRO: Lovely Leonor,
                    are you dressed to go out at this hour?
(*aside*)   How fortunate Celia warned me
                    about her wanting to escape to a convent!
(*aloud*)   Where are you going in such haste?

CASTAÑO (*aside*):   Dear God! He thinks I'm Leonor!
                    I'm done for,
                    if he discovers who I am.

DON PEDRO: What are you afraid of, Leonor?
                    Where are you going, my Leonor?[19]

CASTAÑO (*aside*):   Listen to those "Leonors."
                    But, since he's decided I'm Leonor,
                    I'll pretend to be her.
                    If I speak in a high pitch
                    maybe he won't recognize the voice.

DON PEDRO: Why won't you speak to me, Señora?
                    Is my love not worthy of a
                    response? Why do you want
                    to leave my house? Is it an offense
                    to adore you so tenderly,

to love you so truly?
Although you love another,
I have been attentive to
your obligations,
your honor, and your person,
since I'm determined to marry you
no matter what the cost.
Given your intelligence,
I'm sure that duty
will move you more than the stars
to consider your reputation.
   Is it possible that you aren't moved
by my affection, my nobility,
my estate, or my person,
to judge me less severely?
Supposing I were, Señora,
as unworthy as you think I am,
wouldn't this display of my nobility
give me some grace?
If you're concerned about propriety,
isn't it better to have
a less desirable man who adores you
rather than a more desirable one who spurns
   you?

CASTAÑO (*aside*):   How wonderful to be wooed!
I'm not surprised that
women are so haughty;
nothing makes one so arrogant
as having men begging at your feet!
Well then, reverse direction,
and fire on this fool!
(*aloud*)   —Don Pedro, I wanted to avoid mentioning
my motive, because it's so obvious,
but it seems necessary to state it:
I'm starving to death
because you're so stingy;
and because you're a bastard,
your sister's a meddling hag,
your maids are prudes,

and your servants are pigs.[20]
So I'm leaving this awful house
to go to a pastry shop
to dine on cream puffs.

DON PEDRO (*aside*): What words are these?
How could the brilliant
and beautiful Doña Leonor
speak so crudely?
(*aloud*) —Señora, I am much amazed
to hear you hurl such
terrible insults at my household.
If you wanted to disparage me
you could easily have done it another way,
without demeaning yourself
by using such horrible words.

CASTAÑO: I said I was starving to death,
is that Greek to you?

DON PEDRO: No, it's not Greek to me,
but I don't understand your speaking like that.

CASTAÑO: If you don't understand that,
maybe you'll understand this.

(*He starts to exit.*)

DON PEDRO: Wait! You mustn't go,
nor can I allow you to go alone,
because I told your father
you were here. I'd have to
explain to him later
what happened to you.
Even if you don't want to marry me,
I'll preserve my honor
by returning you to your father,
because the resistance
to the marriage comes from you
and not from me.

CASTAÑO: Don Pedro, you're an idiot.
And it's a great presumption
on your part to prevent
a woman of my talents
from filling her belly.

DON PEDRO (*aside*):   My God, is it possible
that Leonor uses such words?
Dear God, I think she
plays the fool to see
if this will discourage me
and break off the wedding!
God, she hates me! But
even knowing that
can't cool my passion
which loves her blindly.
(*aloud*)   —Lovely Leonor,
why are you pretending to be a fool
when I know how intelligent you are?
Your play-acting only serves to
make me love you even more,
seeing your skill and your wisdom
in knowing how to play the fool.

CASTAÑO (*aside*):   A huge difficulty, by God!
I think he's going to force himself on me right here!
I'd better change styles
to get him to leave me alone.
(*aloud*)   Don Pedro, I'm a woman
who knows where the shoe
pinches; and since I've seen
that your wooing will bear
the weight of my insults,
I want to turn about
and switch sides.
This very night, I
will be your wife.

DON PEDRO: What did you say, Señora?

CASTAÑO: That I'll be yours
as sure as two and two are four.

DON PEDRO: Don't speak in haste.
Happiness may kill me,
even though sorrow could not.

CASTAÑO: Then no, Señor, don't die,
by the love of God,
until you give me a son
to inherit the house.

DON PEDRO: What are you suggesting, Señora?
Everything I have is yours.

CASTAÑO: Damn it, I know what I'm saying.
I need legal guarantees.[21]

DON PEDRO: Nothing would please me more,
but, Señora, are you telling the truth
or toying with my life?

CASTAÑO: Do you think I'm a cheap comedian?
I promise to get married,
unless you don't want it.

DON PEDRO: Me? What do you mean, Señora?

CASTAÑO: I'll bet you that when
the time comes, you'll back down.

DON PEDRO: Don't insult my love like that.

CASTAÑO: Then promise me right now
that if you don't go through with it,
you won't do me any harm.

DON PEDRO: Why is this promise

Trials: Act Three

so important? I believe
it's impossible I'd ever
abandon my darling.
But give me the pleasure
of kissing your beautiful hand
as a pledge of your desire to be my wife.

CASTAÑO (*aside*):   Now this is like the story of Jacob.
(*aloud*)   Here it is; all of it.

DON PEDRO: Would you remove the glove?

CASTAÑO: No, because they're diseased.

DON PEDRO: What is wrong with your hands?

CASTAÑO: They were ruined
one day on a visit,
and not even remedies of
witch hazel or soap
could get them lily white again.

DON JUAN (*off-stage*):   Die by my hand, you traitor!

DON PEDRO: Listen! Whose voice was that?

DON CARLOS (*off-stage*):   You'll die by my hands,
since you seek death in them!

DON PEDRO: My God, what's happening in my house?

CASTAÑO: Now the voice is coming closer.

(*DON CARLOS and DON JUAN enter fighting, and DOÑA ANA enters after them.*)

DOÑA ANA: Gentlemen, stop it!
(*aside*)   It's my brother! I'm dead!

CASTAÑO: Are those suitors

fighting over my beauty?

DON PEDRO: How could two men dare
to duel in my house
during the night?
But I'll avenge this insult
and kill them, especially
since one of them is Don Carlos.

DOÑA ANA (*aside*): How unlucky! Who'd have thought
my brother would be here?

DON CARLOS (*aside*): Don Pedro's here, and
nothing would please me more than to kill him.
But Doña Ana's in danger,
which is all that matters.

CASTAÑO (*aside*): We're under attack!²²
But I'll put out the lights,
then perhaps I might
have time to find the door,
which is all that matters to me.

(*CASTAÑO extinguishes the candle as they all fight.*)

DON PEDRO: Although you've put out the light
to escape my wrath,
it doesn't matter at all to me.
Even in the darkness, I know how to kill you.

DON CARLOS (*aside*): This is an excellent opportunity
for me to save Doña Ana,
since by offering me asylum
she risked her life.

(*DOÑA LEONOR enters wearing her veil.*)

DOÑA LEONOR (*aside*): My God! I left Celia here,
and now I hear the sound of sword fighting
and see only oppressive darkness.

> What is it? God protect me!
> But whatever is happening,
> finding the door
> is all that matters to me.

(*She bumps into DON CARLOS.*)

DON CARLOS (*aside*): This must be Doña Ana.
(*aloud*) —Señora, come quickly.
I'll save you from this danger.

DOÑA LEONOR (*aside*): What is this? A man grabbed me!
But as he says he'll save me,
I'll be grateful whoever he is.
If he mistakes me for someone else,
when he sees me outside
he can leave me there
and return to save her.

DOÑA ANA (*aside*): It doesn't matter to me
that my brother knows about this duel,
especially because he's seen
that Don Carlos is involved;
I'll say that the fight is over Leonor.
All that matters to me
is that Don Carlos is in danger.
If only I could find him
and hide him again!

DON PEDRO: Whoever insults my honor dies!

CASTAÑO: I've lost my bearings
and can't find the door!
It should be here.
Jesus! What is it? A cupboard
which I poked my nose into,
and broke ten dozen
pitchers and vials,
which envious of my beauty
have treated my face vilely.

DOÑA ANA: I heard the sound of a door.[23]
That must have been Don Juan,
leaving so he wouldn't be seen
by my brother who knows him.
Only two are left fighting,
which one is Don Carlos?

DON CARLOS: The door must be here.
Señora, come with me.

(*DON CARLOS exits with DOÑA LEONOR.*)

DON PEDRO: Die by my hand!

DOÑA ANA (*aside*): That's my brother.
This must be Carlos.

(*DOÑA ANA grabs DON JUAN.*)
Come quickly, Señor.
I'll hide you.

DON JUAN (*aside*): That's Doña Ana who wants
to hide me from her brother.
I must obey her.

(*DOÑA ANA exits with DON JUAN.*)

DON PEDRO: Where are you hiding, you cowards,
that my sword cannot find you?
Hey there! Bring in a light!

(*CELIA enters with a light.*)

CELIA: Señor, whose voices were those?

DON PEDRO: See for yourself![24]
(*aside*) But what do I see?
Finding an open door,
they left. But Leonor—
Don Carlos must have come for her—

           Leonor is still in my house,
           which is all that matters to me.
           But it would be good
           to know how he came in.
(*aloud*)   —Leonor, go inside
           and hide. I'll make sure
           your father comes here,
           because I want the wedding
           done tonight.

CASTAÑO: All I want is
           to have my nose fixed.

(*CASTAÑO exits, and DON PEDRO locks the door.*)

DON PEDRO: I want to lock up Leonor
           just in case her choosing me
           was a trick.
           I have to lock her in,
           so if she was play-acting
           the joke will be on her.
           I should find out
           who allowed my rival
           to into my house.
           And why was Carlos fighting
           with that man whose face was hidden?
           Before I saw them
           my sister had seen them, and
           one of them left with her.
           I must know how this all began;
           And where she is and with what man.

(*DON PEDRO exits.*)

SCENE TWO

[ON THE STREET, IN FRONT OF THE HOUSE]

(*DON RODRIGO and HERNANDO enter.*)²⁵

DON RODRIGO: This much I know, Hernando:
    Don Diego was wounded,
    and the man who did it
    led Leonor out of my house.
    Don Diego recognized her and tried to stop her,
    which started the sword fight.
    During the fighting,
    the man who abducted Leonor
    stabbed Don Diego,
    leaving him near death.
    Immediately, Don Diego
    was lifted and carried to his house,
    where he recovered his senses
    as soon as he entered.
    Among the men
    who took pity on him and carried him home,
    Don Diego recognized
    one of Don Pedro's servants.
    Surely Don Pedro had them take him home
    to avoid a disturbance in the street.
        You see how well this matches
    what Don Pedro told me this morning:
    that Leonor only went to see his sister,
    and that I should proceed slowly,
    in order to see if Leonor wants to marry him.
    From this it is clear
    that he intends to delay the marriage
    with these excuses.
    But I have come to his house
    because I am resolved
    to press this advantage
    and force him to marry her
    or kill him immediately.

HERNANDO: You do well, Señor, to apply
a hasty remedy to your wounded honor,
because a foolish delay causes
the wound to continue to fester.

(*DON CARLOS enters with DOÑA LEONOR hidden by a veil.*)²⁶

DON CARLOS: Don't be afraid of the danger,
beautiful Doña Ana.

DOÑA LEONOR (*aside*): My God, does Carlos,
my cruel tormentor, lead me
thinking I'm Doña Ana?
What clearer indication
of his love for her do I need?

DON CARLOS (*aside*): God, what trials
I've experienced
to free Doña Ana,
but left Leonor in danger!
Where can I take her,
so I can return for Leonor
with a clear conscience?
I see a man near by.
(*aloud*) Who goes there?

DON RODRIGO: Is that Don Carlos?

DON CARLOS: I am.
(*aside*) Thank God it's Don Rodrigo!
Who could be better
to entrust with the care
and protection of Doña Ana?
With his age and discretion,
he'll reconcile her to her brother
reasonably. I'll be rid
of this problem and return
to see if I can boldly
rescue my love.

(*aloud*) Señor
Don Rodrigo, I'm in
a quandary, and only you
can help me.

DON RODRIGO: How may I serve you, Don Carlos?

DON CARLOS: This lady who
I brought with me, Señor,
is the sister of Don Pedro.
Due to a disturbance, it was necessary
to take her out of the house,
because her honor was endangered.
You know that it's improper
for me to be with her, so
I beg you to take her to your house,
while I undergo another trial.

DON RODRIGO: Don Carlos, I will take her.
Clearly she should not be alone
with you. And I will speak
to her brother if you wish.

DON CARLOS: Thank you for your help.
And so, I must go.

(*He exits.*)

DOÑA LEONOR (*aside*): What do I see?
He delivered me to my father!

DON RODRIGO: Hernando,
since I am going to see Don Pedro,
and since I know by other signs
that Don Carlos loves his sister,
and that Don Carlos abducted her
as Don Pedro abducted Leonor;
I have decided
to make use of this occasion
to settle this dispute.

Since Don Pedro is to be my son-in-law,
I must see to his honor.
Perhaps seeing his own honor
so exposed to danger will
make him want to restore mine.

HERNANDO: Well said. And it seems to me
a good way of compelling him.
Don't surrender his sister to him
until he's fulfilled
what he promised you.

DON RODRIGO: Then let us go inside.
(*to* DOÑA LEONOR)   Come with me, Señora, without delay,
for I am obliged to help you in every way.

(*They exit.*)

SCENE THREE

[INSIDE THE HOUSE][27]

(*DOÑA LEONOR, DON RODRIGO, and HERNANDO enter.*)

DOÑA LEONOR (*aside*): My father forces me
    to return to my enemy's house,
    and I must follow him
    because I can't reveal who I am.

DON RODRIGO: I see Don Pedro over there.
    —You, Señora, stay here
    with Hernando
    while I speak to your brother.

DOÑA LEONOR (*aside*): Dear God, alter my dark
    destiny, or let me die.
    A quick death, although cruel,
    would be kinder
    than this interminable torture!

DON RODRIGO: I will approach him.

(*DON PEDRO enters.*)

DON PEDRO (*aside*): It angers me
    not to know who allowed
    my rival to enter my house
    and not to find my sister!
    I decided to look for her
    near the garden, for perhaps,
    fearful of the fighting,
    she came to this room.
    But Don Rodrigo is here!
    This is fortunate,
    since Leonor just told me
    that she wants to be my wife.
    —Señor, you have come at the right time.
    You arrive to see me,

Trials: Act Three

       while at the same time
       I was looking for you.

DON RODRIGO: I commend your diligence.
       Please be seated; we have much to discuss.

DON PEDRO (*aside*):   I assume his appearance here
       will bring me my desire.

DON RODRIGO: You may have guessed,
       Don Pedro, that my honor
       brought me here
       since it depends on
       your promise of marriage.
       Because of your high rank,
       my honor will suffer more than yours
       if you refuse to marry her.
       You know that honor is a precious jewel
       that a noble heart
       cannot permit to be put at risk.
       It is a highly polished mirror;
       even though it is not broken,
       the slightest breath can cloud it over.
       You believe this
       and will act on this belief,
       and it brought me here as well.
       But this is not the main reason
       I came. I plan to proceed
       courteously with you;
       in spite of my concerns for
       my daughter and my honor,
       I place your honor above mine.
       I negotiate with you
       with extreme delicacy,
       so that I may increase my honor
       by first securing yours.
       You also increase your honor
       by becoming my son-in-law,
       although I also concede
       that the advantage is mine.

The restoration of your honor
will strengthen mine as well.
If I guard your honor
with such zeal,
how much more zealously
will I guard my own!
    Having said that, you know
that Don Carlos de Olmedo
comes from an illustrious family
of noble birth . . .

DON PEDRO (*aside*):   He mentioned Don Carlos.
Where will this lead?
And why isn't he talking about my marriage?
Clearly, he knows it was
Don Carlos who eloped with Leonor.
I've lost my honor and my life!

DON RODRIGO: You turn pale and
I am not surprised. When hearing
of matters concerning honor,
you would not be noble, prudent,
or honorable, if you did not
show such noble sentiment.
Since your own behavior
serves as an example,
and your own guilt
provokes another crime,
you must not be surprised
that someone has done the same to you.

(*DOÑA ANA enters and hides behind the curtain.*)[28]

DOÑA ANA (*aside*):   Don Rodrigo is with my brother.
From here I'll listen
to find out why he came.
Since Don Carlos is hiding,
and my brother saw him,
everything causes me anxiety.

DON RODRIGO: I say, then, although you may

already be informed of it,
that Don Carlos has
lawfully courted your sister.
As for returning his love, Doña Ana . . .
But that is not surprising,
since you abducted Leonor in the same way.

DON PEDRO: What is this? God forbid!
Does Don Carlos love my sister?

DOÑA ANA (*aside*): How could Don Rodrigo
have come to that conclusion?

DON RODRIGO: I say, without wasting time
on what you already know,
that when Don Carlos discovered the difficulty
of having been seen by you
and having begun a duel with you,
he took her out of your house.

DON PEDRO: What are you saying?

DON RODRIGO: What you did to me
is now happening to you.
Is it possible for you to commit
the same offense against me,
which I have come to discuss
with you so discreetly,
without realizing that Heaven arranges
for the sins we commit against others
to be committed against us?
Take my advice, my son.
When honor is wounded,
it is better to use
mild remedies
rather than harsh ones
that may cause harm.
When a limb is diseased,
the experienced surgeon
does not use the knife
and sever the painful limb,

without first trying
a soothing balm.
He comes to more drastic measures
only when it is recognized
that there is no other way.
So it must be with us.
Don Carlos spoke to me of her,
Doña Ana was with him,
and I have her now.
They acted without you . . .
But since they have already done it,
let it be with your blessing,
discreetly and carefully,
consenting to what must be.
It is a clever man
who dresses necessity
in the clothes of inclination.
That is my advice.
Now think carefully
about your honor, and you will see
what the proper course of action is.
    And in considering what concerns me,
know that I am determined
that you will be married tonight.
There is no reason to hesitate,
since I discovered
that you wounded Don Diego last night
because he recognized you and
wanted to prevent you from abducting Leonor.
You see how this contradicts
the story you invented.
It is, in all, a large debt.
Only by marrying her
can you settle all accounts.

DOÑA ANA (*aside*):   I'm eager to hear my brother's
response. But I don't understand
what motive could have caused
Don Rodrigo to fabricate
this elaborate lie.

DON PEDRO: Señor, first of all,
I want to say that when I denied
I abducted Leonor, it was a white lie
told to protect my honor
and your reputation.
You say I can settle accounts
only by marrying her.
The lovely Leonor
is hidden in that room.
And now in your presence
I swear to be her husband and master.
But you must know
that my primary concern
is Doña Ana. Therefore,
I'll follow your advice
and give her to Don Carlos
immediately.
(*aside*)   With this,
I'm sure to foil my rival
in every possible way.

DON RODRIGO: In this, you demonstrate
your nobility and your prudence!
I will bring your sister here
and give her the good news.

(*DOÑA ANA comes out from behind the curtain.*)

DOÑA ANA: There's no need for that, Don Rodrigo.
I owe you much more
than I could ever say.
—And you, my brother, although
I deserve your wrath, I beg you
to reflect in your heart
on the violence of your own passion
and forgive my sins;
if indeed I am guilty
of any crime but love.

DON PEDRO: Rise, Doña Ana.

> Your marriage could have been
> arranged more properly
> without resorting
> to such indecent behavior.

DON RODRIGO: Stop there. This is no time
for reprimands. Send
a servant of yours
to go in search of Don Carlos.

DOÑA ANA: There isn't any need to send anyone,
since I've hidden him in my room
as if he were my husband.

DON PEDRO: Bring him here immediately.

DOÑA ANA I obey with pleasure.
Finally my love succeeds
in gaining its desire!

(She exits.)

DON PEDRO: Celia!

(CELIA enters.)

CELIA: What is your command?

DON PEDRO: Take the key to that room
and tell Leonor to come out.
Oh Love, finally in my eagerness
you have granted success
to my loving heart!

(CELIA takes the key and exits.)

DOÑA LEONOR *(aside)*:[29] Since they thought I was Doña
Ana,
I'm free to go inside
and escape from my father,

who's the greatest danger,
and later I'll find a way
to escape from
Don Pedro's pleading.
But I see a man climbing
up the stairs. Who is it?

(*DON CARLOS enters.*)

DON CARLOS (*aside*): Against all odds, I come
determined to rescue Leonor
from this shameful captivity.
Assuming that Doña Ana
has escaped the danger,
there's no longer any reason
to hide my actions.
God grant that I find her,
or I must die here!

(*DON CARLOS passes by DOÑA LEONOR.*)

DOÑA LEONOR (*aside*): My God, it's Carlos,
so blinded by passion
that he didn't see me.
Perhaps he realized he left
his love in danger
and returned to rescue her.
Oh God! You've brought me here
to confirm his cruelty!
But if he thought he
freed his lady from her trials
and escaped with her,
why has he returned? I'll go closer
to hear what he says.

DON CARLOS: Don Pedro, when entering
my enemy's house,
I cannot be expected to act courteously.
You have my . . . But what do I see?
Is Don Rodrigo here?

DON RODRIGO: Keep still, Don Carlos, and be quiet,
    because all your trials
    are ended. Don Pedro
    grants what you desire.
    Show him your gratitude
    for you owe him much.
    I congratulate you
    on becoming the fortunate owner
    of the beauty you adore.
    May you enjoy her forever.

DON CARLOS (*aside*): What is this? Clearly,
    he knows what happened,
    so Castaño must have
    given him my letter.
    Knowing that I am the one who eloped with
      Leonor,
    Don Rodrigo wants to act
    prudently and give Leonor to me,
    and clearly Don Pedro,
    learning the truth,
    stopped pursuing her.
(*aloud*) —Señor, I don't know how
    to begin to answer you.
    But allow my happiness
    to excuse my foolishness.
    I didn't expect to earn
    such good fortune.
    I'd be a little mad,
    if I weren't delirious.

DON RODRIGO (*to* DON PEDRO): What did I tell you?
    He loves her passionately.

DOÑA LEONOR (*aside*): Dear God, what do I hear?
    Why do they congratulate him,
    and why is Don Carlos so happy?

DON PEDRO: Although it would have been prudent
    for you to have

discussed this with me,
Don Rodrigo, whose gray hairs
I honor as my father's,
desires the match,
so I consider myself fortunate
to have such an esteemed gentleman
as a member of my family.

DOÑA LEONOR (*aside*):   I won't endure it!
The traitor won't marry her!

(*DOÑA LEONOR steps forward, still hidden behind her veil.*)

DON RODRIGO: Señora, you come at a
very opportune moment.
But why are you wearing a veil
as if to go outside now?
—Don Carlos, dispense with the courtesies;
give your hand to Doña Ana.

DON CARLOS: To whom? What is this?

DON RODRIGO: To Doña Ana, your wife.
What disturbs you?

DON CARLOS: God help me! I'm betrayed
by a trick. I? Marry Doña Ana?

DOÑA LEONOR (*aside*):   Thank God he scorns her!

DON PEDRO: Don Rodrigo, what's this?
Didn't you come to negotiate
for my sister on behalf
of Don Carlos?

DON RODRIGO: Of course.
Because Don Carlos himself
entrusted your sister to me
and brought her to me,
saying that he had taken her

because her life was in danger.
—Señora, is this not so?

DOÑA LEONOR: Yes, Señor, and I confess
I will be Carlos' wife,
if you agree to it.

DON CARLOS: Señora Doña Ana, you behave
very badly in exposing yourself
to such public humiliation
as I by force must do to you,
for you oblige me
to speak discourteously to you.
Since you exhaust my patience,
you must endure my harsh words.
You should know better than
anyone else that I
can never stop loving Leonor.

DON RODRIGO: Leonor? What? How can that be?
What Leonor?

DON CARLOS: Your daughter.

DON RODRIGO: My daughter? It cannot be,
since she is Pedro's wife!

DON CARLOS: I would kill him
before I'd let him marry Leonor!

DON PEDRO: I've suffered too much already,
since in my presence you boldly and rudely
scorned my sister and
declared your love for my wife!

(*They draw their swords. DOÑA ANA and DON JUAN enter hand in hand.*)

DOÑA ANA: Brother, we kneel at your feet,
my husband and I . . .
(*aside*) But what do I see?

> I must have led Don Juan here.
> I didn't recognize him
> with his face hidden by his cloak.[30]

DON PEDRO: Doña Ana, what's the meaning of this?

(CELIA *enters from the opposite side of the stage with* CASTAÑO *still dressed as a woman.*)

CELIA: Señor, here's Doña Leonor.

DON PEDRO: My beautiful, divine mistress!

CASTAÑO: I don't know about my beauty,
but I'm frozen with fear.
But my lover's here,
so nothing frightens me,
since he'll protect me.

DON RODRIGO: I do not believe what I see.
—Don Carlos, was it not Doña Ana
who you entrusted to me,
and who you will marry?

DON CARLOS: Clearly, it was a trick,
for I love only Leonor.

DOÑA ANA (*aside*): This unmasking destroys
my determined design.
This must be Don Juan.
I must try any way I can
to respect him, since
he will be my master in the end.
(*aside*) —Don Rodrigo, what are you saying?
I know nothing about Don Carlos.
I only know that since I left Madrid
Don Juan reigned absolutely
over all the thoughts
in my heart.

DON JUAN: Don Pedro, I kneel at your feet.

DON PEDRO: I am the one who should rejoice,
              since my friend joins my family.
              So, in order for our weddings
              to take place at the same time,
              give your hand to Doña Ana
              as I offer mine to Leonor.

(*He crosses to* CASTAÑO.)

DON CARLOS: I'll kill you first!

CASTAÑO (*aside*): I'm so handsome,
              they want to die for me.

DON PEDRO: Queen of my heart,
              yield to my love
              and grant me your hand in marriage.

CASTAÑO: I will, but even cheap gloves[31]
              would be softer
              than the hand I grant you.

DON CARLOS: You can't have her!

(*DOÑA LEONOR removes her veil.*)

DOÑA LEONOR: Be still, Carlos! I waited
              too long, and I will be your wife.
              Although you seemed to scorn me,
              I naturally love you
              even more for it.

DON CARLOS: Leonor, my love, is that you?

DON PEDRO: What is this? Could it be a dream?
              Is Leonor both here and there?

CASTAÑO: No. Now it's my cue to say:
              You are not yourself, Leonor . . .

Trials: Act Three 145

DON PEDRO: Then, who are you, miraculous beauty,
who I mistook for Leonor?

(*CASTAÑO removes his disguise.*)

CASTAÑO: I'm only a cheap trick[32]
in gloves.

CELIA: I can't stop laughing
at Castaño's trick.

DON PEDRO: By God, I'll kill you!

CASTAÑO: Why? I promised
to marry you, and
I'm ready to do it.
We made an agreement
that if you abandoned me,
you wouldn't hurt me.
You gave your word,
and I'm ready to do my part.
You can't break your promise,
since I won't break mine.

DON CARLOS: What is this, Castaño,
and why are you dressed like that?

CASTAÑO: This is my disguise
for taking the letter
which I have kept here
in which you told
Don Rodrigo the whole story
about you eloping with Leonor.
I put on this disguise
so that I could deliver it
without risking an encounter with the police.
Don Pedro, falling in love
with my figure, my hair style,

my grace, and my elegance,
locked me in that room.

DON CARLOS: You see for yourself, Don Rodrigo,
it's true that I'm
the man Leonor loves,[33]
and I should be her husband.

DON RODRIGO: As long as Leonor is married,
and my honor is not tarnished,
nothing else matters to me.
So, Don Carlos, I am happy
to have acquired such a son-in-law.

DON PEDRO (*aside*): My God! I'm so embarrassed
this happened to me;
I don't know what to say.
I must swallow my pride,
since I can't do anything about it.
(*aloud*) I'll accept that
a good joke was played on me,
because my sister will marry
Don Juan.

DOÑA ANA: I offer my hand,
and with it my heart.

DON JUAN: And I, Señora, accept it,
securing my future
by offering mine to you.

DON CARLOS: My Leonor, give me your hand.

DOÑA LEONOR: I don't have it to give,
for it has always been yours.

CASTAÑO: Look around, Celia,
and see if you have
a hand that's handy.

CELIA: I don't know if I
 can afford to give you my hand.[34]
 Would my finger be enough for you?

CASTAÑO: Give it here, since I find you
 attached to it.
(*to the audience*)
 We're all paired up for walking down the aisles,
 so now we shut the door on *The House of Trials*.[35]

Notes for Act III

1 Again, Celia uses the word *tramoya*, which means stage machinery as well as a trick.

2 A few scholars cite this passage as autobiographical proof of an unhappy love affair causing Sor Juana to enter a convent. The allusion is more likely another ironic in-joke about Sor Juana's vocation in general rather than a reference to a specific event in her life.

3 The original allusion is to a medieval romance in which Melisandra, the daughter of Charlemagne, was held captive by a Moorish king, Marsilio, for seven years until her husband, Gayferos, rescued her. Celia's remark about warning Marsilio of Melisandra's attempt to escape is ironic, since it suggests that Pedro is the villain, while Carlos and Leonor belong together as husband and wife.

4 In spite of Juan's convoluted questioning of the honor code, he decides to follow it and seeks revenge for the assumed affront to his honor.

5 Literally, "honor, incite me to vengeance" or "honor, encourage me to defend myself." Honor in Golden Age drama is not merely public reputation, but also personal dignity, self-worth, and integrity. Since loss of honor is equated with loss of identity, Juan believes he defends his life when he defends his honor.

6 According to an early Christian legend told in *The Acts of Paul and Tecla*, Tecla (or Thecla) of Iconium heard Saint Paul preach and rejected her family and fiancé to follow his teachings on chastity. Powerful men desired her wherever she travelled, and Tecla's life and virginity were preserved only by divine intervention.

7 Garatuza was the pseudonym of Martín de Villavicencio y Salazar, a rogue who passed himself off as a priest in New Spain and was condemned to death in 1648.

8 Some critics point to Castaño's country of origin as the only evidence of the author's *mexicanidad* (Mexican heritage).

9 In other words, whether you are a woman or a man.

10 Sor Juana's play adopts the style and plot devices of Pedro Calderón de la Barca, the most famous Spanish playwright of the late seventeenth century. After acknowledging her debt to him, she then borrows a plot device rarely used by Calderón.

11 Castaño describes himself as a *morena*, a dark-haired woman, instead of as a *moreno*, a dark-haired man.

12 Castaño mentions a *pechuguera*, which must be derived from *pecho* (chest), although Celsa Carmen García Valdés notes that the word does not appear in any dictionary (236). It may be what the eighteenth-century French called a *modestie*, a piece of lace or diaphanous fabric that covered the bosom in a low neckline.

13 Although asides are always given directly to the audience, as if characters are speaking to sympathetic peers, this is the first aside in which the audience is addressed "by name." It is not clear whether Sor Juana expects her audience to be entirely female or if she addresses the women in a mixed audience.

14 Literally, Castaño refers to *sacristanes*, metal cages used to support the skirts like Elizabethan farthingales. Note that in Act I (note 22) Castaño said he expected to find sanctuary in a *sacristán*.

15 In Chapter 27 of Genesis, young Jacob fooled his blind father, Isaac, into thinking he was his hairy brother, Esau, by covering his smooth hands and arms with goatskins.

16 A *foso* can be either a pit or a cellar under a stage.

17 This is the pseudonym for Antonio María de Benavides, an adventurer who pretended to be the Marquis of San Vicente and an official appointed by the Spanish king. He was prosecuted and hanged in 1684, a year after the play was written.

18 Castaño refers to an official, possibly the Viceroy or Vicereine, who was present when *The House of Trials* was first performed.

19 Pedro uses the familiar form of you in this speech, but returns to the formal form in the next speech.

20 Literally, Castaño says, "because you are unfortunate, your sister is a mother-in-law, your maids are aunts, and your servants are beasts."

21 Since women did not automatically inherit property from their husbands in the seventeenth century, they needed sons to inherit the estate and provide for them in their old age.

22 Literally, he says "Here it is like Oran," a Spanish city in North Africa which was repeatedly attacked by the Moors in the seventeenth century.

23 Apparently, she hears Castaño shut the cupboard door.

24 Literally, he exclaims "What should it be!" meaning he thinks he knows who they are.

25 Again, Sor Juana departs from the usual *romance* to render the dialogue between Rodrigo and Hernando in rhymed couplets, *pareados*, continuing the pattern of switching to stricter verse forms whenever Rodrigo enters.

26 The verse changes from *pareados* to *romances*, signaling a change from discussion to action.

27 There is no break in the action even though the setting changes. This dramaturgical technique is rare in English drama of the period, but not uncommon in Spanish Golden Age drama.

28 A curtain (*paño*) hung at the rear of Spanish Golden Age stages. Scripts indicate that a character hides behind the curtain by noting that the character is *al paño*.

29 Leonor has remained hidden through-out the scene.

30 In production, Juan wore a mask in the last act, and this line was changed to "with his face hidden behind a mask."

31 Castaño describes the gloves as *de perro* (made from a dog), which is a slang expression meaning lousy or filthy.

32 Literally, Castaño says, "I'm only the dead dog from whom the gloves were made." The phrase *el perro muerto*, which means "the dead dog," could also mean "the bed trick" in seventeenth-century Spanish. Bed tricks (when people are tricked into having sex with someone other than the person they expect) are used by Shakespeare in *Measure for Measure* and *All's Well that Ends Well*. In Tirso de Molina's play, *El burlador de Sevilla* (*The Trickster of Seville*), Don Juan asks the Marqués de Mota about his *perros muertos*, in which Mota tricks prostitutes into sleeping with his friends while the women mistakenly believe they are sleeping with Mota (see Act Two, line 206). With the phrase *el perro muerto*, Castaño also makes a reference to his previous allusion to the gloves being *de perro*. Unfortunately, no English expression can convey both puns.

33 Literally, "I am the master of Leonor's beauty."

34 Literally, Celia says, "I left my *mano* in the kitchen." *Mano* usually means hand, but it also means a pestle or other grinding instrument.

35 Most Spanish Golden Age plays end with an apology for any faults the actors may have committed and a request for applause.

Ibérica

This series of scholarly monographs focuses upon sixteenth- and seventeenth-century Hispanic Theater. *Ibérica* welcomes historical and cultural studies as well as theoretical and critical texts that would enhance our understanding of the *Comedia* as a European phenomenon. Manuscripts may be in English, Spanish or Portuguese, with a minimum of 200 pages. Inquires and manuscripts should be directed to the General Editor:

> A. Robert Lauer
> Dept. of Modern Languages,
>   Literature & Linguistics
> University of Oklahoma
> 780 Van Vleet Oval, Room 202
> Norman, OK 73019